FEMININITY AND THE PHYSICALLY ACTIVE WOMAN

Femininity and the Physically Active Woman explores one reason many women offer for their lack of involvement in sport and exercise – that they are not the 'sporty' type. Precilla Y. L. Choi argues that the 'sporty' type is masculine, and to determine how this notion might affect women's self-perceptions, she critically examines the experiences of women athletes, bodybuilders, recreational exercisers and girls' physical education. What emerges is the importance of visible differences between women and men, in terms of muscularity, strength and agility in order to maintain the gender order. Thus, if a girl or woman wishes to play the masculine game of sport she must do so in conformity with a number of patriarchal rules which ensure she is first and foremost recognised as a heterosexual feminine being.

Contributing to a psychology of the physically active woman by examining women's experiences from critical feminist and gendered perspectives, *Femininity and the Physically Active Woman* will be of great interest to students, researchers, practitioners and teachers from a range of disciplines.

Precilla Y. L. Choi is a Senior Lecturer in Psychology at Keele University and the British Association for the Advancement of Science's Joseph Lister Lecturer for 2000. She has co-edited, with Paula Nicolson, *Female Sexuality* (Prentice Hall).

WOMEN AND PSYCHOLOGY
Series Editor: Jane Ussher
Centre for Critical Psychology,
University of Western Sydney

This series brings together current theory and research on women and psychology. Drawing on scholarship from a number of different areas of psychology, it bridges the gap between abstract research and the reality of women's lives by integrating theory and practice, research and policy.

Each book addresses a 'cutting edge' issue of research, covering such topics as post-natal depression, eating disorders, theories and methodologies.

The series provides accessible and concise accounts of key issues in the study of women and psychology, and clearly demonstrates the centrality of psychology to debates within women's studies or feminism.

The Series Editor would be pleased to discuss proposals for new books in the series.

Other titles in this series:

THIN WOMAN
Helen Malson

THE MENSTRUAL CYCLE
Anne E. Walker

POST-NATAL DEPRESSION
Paula Nicolson

RE-THINKING ABORTION
Mary Boyle

WOMEN AND AGING
Linda R. Gannon

BEING MARRIED, DOING GENDER
Caroline Dryden

UNDERSTANDING DEPRESSION
Janet M. Stoppard

FEMININITY AND THE PHYSICALLY ACTIVE WOMAN

Precilla Y. L. Choi

London and Philadelphia

First published 2000
by Routledge
11 New Fetter Lane, London EC4P 4EE

Simultaneously published in the USA and Canada
by Taylor and Francis Inc
325 Chestnut Street, Suite 800, Philadelphia, PA 19106

Routledge is an imprint of the Taylor and Francis Group

© 2000 Precilla Choi

Typeset in Sabon by M Rules
Printed and bound in Great Britain by
Biddles Ltd, www. biddles.co.uk

British Library Cataloguing in Publication Data
A catalogue record for this book is available from the British Library

ISBN 0-415-16560-1 (hbk)
ISBN 0-415-16561-X (pbk)

FOR THE KRALING FAMILY
WITH THANKS

CONTENTS

CONTENTS

FIGURES

ACKNOWLEDGEMENTS

The writing of the book was funded, in part, by a Nuffield Foundation Science Research Fellowship awarded in 1995. I am also grateful to Bowling Green State University's School of Human Movement and Leisure Studies, USA, for hosting me during my sabbatical in 1999 and to Keele University's Psychology Department for their support, especially Jane Ginsborg and Susan O'Neill.

Throughout the process of producing this book I was privileged to receive much intellectual and emotional support from many friends and colleagues. In particular, I would like to thank the following for putting up with my bad moods and/or reading chapters and offering constructive criticism: Kate Bennett, Melanie Bishop, Ros Bramwell, Dereth Carr, Louise Dye, Linda Gannon, Jan Hadlow, Carol Henshaw, Vikki Krane, Nanette Mutrie, Paula Nicolson, Ann Owen, Marian Pitts, John Plummer, Olga Van Den Akker, and Jane Ussher.

Thanks also to John Plummer for the photographs of female bodybuilders (Figures 4.1 and 4.2); to Channel 4 News for allowing me to quote from their news report of the WNBA; to Open University Press for permission to reprint Ajzen's (1988) theory of planned behaviour (Figure 6.1); and to John Wiley & Sons for permission to reprint Eccles et al's (1998) model of achievement choices (Figure 6.2).

1

THE GENDERED NATURE OF
SPORT AND EXERCISE

Ever since I was a child I have been physically very active. At school I competed in dance, swimming, ball sports and athletics events, as a teenager I studied martial arts, competing at regional and national level, and in my twenties I lifted weights, competing in local powerlifting and bodybuilding events. Now, in my late thirties, I no longer compete but continue to participate in various sports and physical activities at a recreational level. Amongst my childhood and adolescent memories are those of my mother asking me the question 'why?' This question seemed to be asked of everything I wanted to do including taking part in my chosen sports. Being questioned led me to believe that what I wanted to do was not acceptable for some reason. This was never the case with my brothers. They were not questioned and they appeared, to me, to be able to have as much fun as they wanted, going where they wanted, doing what they wanted. It seemed that as a girl I was expected to behave differently from my brothers. As a Chinese girl growing up in a white society, I was also somewhat different to my white peers. Of course at the time I did not understand why I was being treated differently from my brothers, nor could I understand why my mother did not understand why I wanted to take part in sport and exercise – but now I do.

Outside of the home I discovered that the insistent questioning was to continue and that whilst at times there was a racial basis for this, it was actually far less frequent than gender. For example, although I was encouraged to play table tennis at school because it was thought that Chinese people had a special talent for this sport, such instances of racial bias were quite rare. Instead, my not being allowed to play soccer was because kicking was considered unladylike and in spite of being Chinese, I was never encouraged to participate in martial arts (fighting is also unladylike). In contrast, because martial arts originate from the East and at the time were popularised by movies starring the Chinese Kung Fu star Bruce Lee, my brothers were expected to excel at this. The questioning, therefore, had a much more major basis in gender. Furthermore, the questioning came in many different guises: not being allowed to play football at school, the indifference of my fellow

1

male martial artists in the dojo, the hostility of the men in the gym – all leading me to question myself. Should I not be here? Am I not good enough? Do I not train hard enough? After all, I was one of very few females, if any, in the dojo or the gym and people often expressed surprise when informed that I participated in these activities.

I also discovered that, whilst participating in my chosen sports and physical activities, I attracted much unwanted sexual attention. As I ran in the streets or the playing fields, as I lifted weights in the gym, as I walked to the starting block at the swimming pool, I endured what I now know to be sexual harassment. During aerobics sessions I endured the men who had gathered to watch as we bent, stretched and jumped up and down. It did not take long for it to become obvious to me that when men exercised or played sport, they did so without being questioned and without having to endure unwanted sexual attention. They were not seen primarily as sexual beings. As with my brothers, I was questioned but they were not. The simple reason for this is gender. That is, the traditional notions of masculinity and femininity which are taught to us from the time we are born through the different ways that we are treated according to whether we are a boy or a girl.

This book, therefore, is about what femininity means in a sport and exercise context. It aims to move beyond mere description of the inequalities that women face in the spheres of sport and exercise and show how gendering continues to maintain the inequalities by mitigating against girls' and women's development as physically active beings. My starting points are the public health data showing that (a) people in general are not taking part in enough physical activity to afford significant health benefits and (b) this is more of a problem for women than men. Given the evidence that links appropriate levels of physical activity with reduced depression and anxiety and increased psychological well-being, together with decreased risk of all cause mortality, incidence of coronary heart disease, colon cancer and diabetes (Pate et al, 1995; US Surgeon General, 1996), these findings constitute a public health problem. We need to understand how and why this low level of physical activity came (and comes) about if measures are to be taken to help increase it.

How much physical activity do people participate in?

Prior to the 1960s physical exercise was about competitive sport – something that was reserved for the elite: young and talented people who strove to attain high levels of physical fitness and participated in events such as the Olympics, Wimbledon and football leagues. At the beginning of the 1960s, this perspective began to change. The Council of Europe developed the 'Sport for All' initiative and moderate physical exercise was promoted as a behaviour important for physical and psychological health. Thus, physical fitness became associated with health.

We can see how this caused a shift in people's thinking about physical exercise and fitness by looking at how definitions of health have expanded or changed to accommodate accepted cultural and societal norms. In an early study Bauman (1961) asked people what being healthy meant to them and found that one dimension of health was indeed considered to be fitness but this was conceptualised as being physically fit enough to perform work tasks and general day to day activities (the other two dimensions were a general sense of well-being and an absence of symptoms of disease). However, in a later study of 9,000 people asked to describe a very healthy person, an additional physical fitness dimension emerged which related to playing sports or taking part in physical exercise (Blaxter, 1990). Being able to participate in these activities was also seen as an indicator of good health, in addition to being physically fit enough to perform one's duties. Thus, as physical fitness became culturally associated with health, people's conceptions of fitness were extended to accommodate this.

It may not be surprising, therefore, to learn that in Britain during the 1980s and 1990s, more people than ever participated in sport and physical exercise. In 1990, the percentage of women and men participating in Great Britain was 39% and 58% respectively (OPCS, 1992); in 1993 the figures were 52% and 72% respectively (OPCS, 1995) and in 1996 the figures were 58% and 71% respectively (OPCS, 1998). These figures appear to mean good news for the health of the British nation. However, these percentages represent people who reported participating in 'some sport or physical activity during the four weeks before interview' (OPCS, 1998; p. 209). Overall this was 64% and as likely to include individuals who went for a leisure walk once in the previous four weeks as those individuals who had run several miles regularly each week. We do not know from this data, therefore, how many people are actually taking part in sufficient exercise to afford significant health benefits. According to the Allied Dunbar National Fitness Survey (ADNFS, 1992), the answer is not enough[1] and what is even more worrying is that this has been found to be more of a problem for women than for men. In the largest UK study of this nature, more than 4,000 people over 16 years old were interviewed in their own homes and 70% of them appraised in an exercise physiology laboratory. The ADNFS found that 7 out of 10 men and 8 out of 10 women of all ages exercise less than the age appropriate requirement for health benefits. These figures are worse amongst the 16–24 year olds where 91% of the women were below the target activity level. Some alarming figures were also found in the older age group – 30% of men and 50% of women aged 65–74 did not have sufficient muscle strength to lift 50% of their body weight. What this means is that they would find it difficult to do a simple task such as rising from a sitting position in a chair or from the floor without using their arms to help them. Another simple fitness test revealed that, of all ages, one third of the men and two thirds of the women were unable to continue at

3

a reasonable pace up a 1 in 20 slope without becoming uncomfortably breathless.

The statistics from USA and Canada are not any better. The US Surgeon General (1996) reported that more than 60% of adults do not achieve the recommended amount of regular physical activity, with 25% not being active at all. This report also highlighted how women of all ages are less active than men. According to Vertinsky (1997) only 12% of the US population and 15% of Canadians report levels of activity that are sufficient for health benefits, with girls and women reporting less than boys and men. She also notes that, in general, physical activity amongst girls declines by almost 50% when they reach adolescence and that the majority of women over the age of 65 do not engage in any systematic exercise. US statistics also indicate that people of colour exercise less than white Americans, with the difference greater for women (Kriska and Rexroad, 1998).

Why are fewer women than men physically active?

A whole host of factors influence people's non-involvement in sport and exercise, from lack of provision to insufficient time or money, but even when people overcome the barriers and begin an exercise programme, they appear to experience great difficulty continuing with it (Biddle, 1995). Again, this is more of a problem for women than for men (ADNFS, 1992). Why are fewer women than men physically active? The ADNFS (1992) found that women, but not men, reported household and caring responsibilities to be a barrier – a disappointing finding in an era when women supposedly have greater equality than ever before. Clearly we have some way to go to achieving total equality in this arena. Just how far is obvious from this statement by an eminent (male) epidemiologist advocating more physical activity for women: 'Ideally, you should stay on your feet for at least an hour a day – chasing the kids, vacuuming or climbing stairs.' (Ralph Paffenbarger, quoted in an article in the magazine *American Health*, September 1995, pp. 38–40.) An esteemed medical scientist such as Paffenbarger could have used the article as an opportunity to recommend that men do their share of the household and caring duties so that women get time to exercise. Instead, however, he reinforces the traditional view that women spend most of their time in the sphere of domestic responsibility with less opportunity than men to take part in activities outside of the home such as sport.

Sociological research has also highlighted barriers to women exercising. These include inadequate street lighting, poor public transport, a lack of child care facilities as well as race and religious factors such as strict codes of dress (Green et al, 1987). Providers of sport and recreation at national, regional and local levels have taken these on board and worked towards addressing them (Women's Sports Foundation, 1995). However, one barrier that does not appear to have been addressed yet is the belief by many women that sport and exercise is not for them. This belief was reflected in the findings of the Blaxter (1990) study above where being fit, in addition to being defined as the ability to perform daily activities, was also defined as being able to take part in sport and physical exercise. However, this dimension of fitness was most often cited by young male respondents and usually described a man, which suggests that both women and men consider sport and exercise related fitness to be more salient to men's health than to women's. This is further supported by the ADNFS research finding that more women than men reported not being the 'sporty' type as a reason for their non-participation in physical exercise. If physical activity is to be increased amongst women, two questions need to be answered: what is the sporty type and how does this affect women's perceptions of themselves as physically active beings.[2]

The 'sporty' type

I wish to argue that the answers to these questions are that the sporty type is masculine and that in addition to the many barriers that people face in taking up and maintaining a physical exercise programme, for girls and women, gender creates additional barriers. When Paula Newby-Fraser won the female triathlon world championship in 1988 she remarked that she did not know that women could go as fast as she did. Why not when she knew that men could? One answer may be that girls and women have been taught, through the process of gendering, that they cannot. This process begins in childhood with the traditional notions of masculinity and femininity that are taught to us and subsequently help to shape our view of and make sense of the world around us. For example, little girls are carried more than little boys and are not allowed to walk and explore alone as much as boys (Lewis, 1972; Mitchell et al, 1992). They are dressed in more delicate and restrictive clothing (Fagot and Leinbach, 1987; Pomerleau et al, 1990), discouraged from engaging in 'rough and tumble'/aggressive play (Di Pietro, 1981; Hyde, 1996), responded to more quickly (Condry et al, 1983) and considered to need more care (Condry and Condry, 1976). For today's adult women the toys and games that were considered more appropriate for them as girls were those that encouraged nurturance behaviour, activities in the home, more physical proximity and more verbal interaction (Caldera et al, 1989). This contributes to children learning that femininity (i.e. being female) means being helpless, incompetent, dependent, nurturant and physically inactive. In contrast, boys learn that masculinity means being independent, able, competent and physically active. Furthermore, through parental encouragement to play with gender appropriate toys (Caldera et al, 1989) girls learn to be concerned with physical appearance, attractiveness and fashion by playing with dolls whilst boys learn to be active and mobile by playing with cars and trucks (Liss, 1983; O'Brien and Huston, 1985). It is not surprising, then, that differences between boys and girls have been observed from a very early age, with boys being more physically active and adventurous than girls (Ryan, 1985). Furthermore, new data has revealed that many parents continue to think that their sons are more interested in and better at sport than their daughters (Eccles, 1999). As a result, they sign the boys up for more sports/physical activities, take them to sports events more often and buy them more sports clothing and equipment. With their daughters, more time is spent reading. These findings have important implications given the research that has found parental (and other adult) support and encouragement to be significant predictors of children's physical activity (Anderssen and Wold, 1992; Stucky-Ropp and DiLorenzo, 1993; Biddle and Goudas, 1996) and that children's appraisal of their ability tends to be congruent with their parents' appraisals (Jacobs and Eccles, 1992; Brustad, 1996).

Stories and fairytales also teach children about gender appropriate behaviour (Ussher, 1997). The traditional stories and fairytales that taught me and my generation about gender appropriate behaviour, and are still popular amongst today's children, illustrate the young and beautiful girl waiting to be rescued by a handsome man. While she lies sleeping (passivity) he fights his way through dense forests or climbs up towers (active), he gazes upon her and finds her beautiful and desirable in her passive state, he kisses her, she wakes up, falls in love and they live happily ever after, he having saved her from her life of misery. In these narratives, the girl is always white, she is always beautiful, she is always helpless and it is always a (white) man with whom she lives happily ever after. Independence, competence, sport, different skin colour and sexual orientation never feature.

In learning to associate sport behaviour with being a man, physical competence becomes an important indicator of masculinity (Connell, 1983). Sports have thus become, for boys and men, a way of constructing a masculine identity (Messner, 1992; Lorber, 1993) and of finding male solidarity (Dunning, 1986). The answer, therefore, to the first question, 'what is the sporty type?' is that the sporty type is masculine. But how can this still be true in the Just Do It era of Girl Power, Sporty Spice and The Can Do Girls? After all, it is certainly the case that women have taken and continue to take their rightful place in the previously exclusive male preserve of sport in growing numbers. Indeed, at the 2000 Olympic Games in Sydney, for the first time in the history of the Olympic movement, almost all events were open to both women and men. With eight more sports opened to women, this makes it a total of 26 of the 28 sports open to men (boxing and wrestling are the remaining two). In addition to events like the Olympic Games there has also been major growth for women in other sporting arenas. For example, in the summer of 1997 women's professional basketball in the USA was, for the first time, televised on American network TV in the same way that men's professional basketball has been for many years.

This Women's National Basketball Association (WNBA) league marked a major breakthrough for women's basketball (and women's sport) in America and the athletes are considered to be the beneficiaries of America's 1972 Title IX government law that prohibits sex discrimination in any educational programme or activity provided by government funded institutions. Whilst directed at education in general, Title IX is thought to have had the greatest impact on women's sport, with significantly expanded opportunities for participation (Greendorfer, 1998). In a news report that appeared on UK's Channel 4 during the summer of 1997 the female athlete was celebrated with one WNBA basketball player saying:

> Who's really going to benefit are the little girls growing up now, watching us play and believing that they can be whatever they want to be. Believing they can be professional athletes. It's exciting. It's an exciting time to be a woman athlete, it's an exciting time to be a sports fan.
>
> (UK Channel 4 News, 18 July 1997)

Thus, whilst once upon a time in the history of women, serious debate took place about whether or not she should participate in sport, it would now seem that the debate has become irrelevant. However, although positive about the WNBA and about women's sports, the Channel 4 news report above very much emphasised the glamour and beauty of the basketball players. To the interviewer's questions about their image, one player replies:

> I think that women are women. Outside the court they can be feminine, you know. They've got their hair, make-up, whatever, but once you step on the court it's a totally different ball game. I know I'm like that myself, you know. If I'm off the court I want to look nice, I want to represent myself and my team well, but when you step on the court, you know, it's time for business.
>
> (UK Channel 4 News, 18 July 1997)

We are thus assured that although she sweats and looks dishevelled when playing basketball, off court she is still concerned with her appearance. It would seem that whilst the female athlete is now acceptable, what remains questionable and relevant is the relationship between femininity and physical activity.

Another example of this is a conversation I found myself having with a group of British friends during the summer of 1999 that concerned the female athlete's behaviour. The topic was Wimbledon as this tennis event was taking place at the time. The conversation began with one of the men in the group saying how he much preferred women's tennis to men's, which led to a discussion of who we thought were the best players and so on. Somehow the conversation turned to women tennis players who grunted when they hit the ball, with some of the group making negative comments about this. When I asked if grunting in male tennis players was also worthy of comment the answer was no although no one could quite articulate to me why not. Again, the female athlete is accepted but the traditional ideology of femininity influences how her behaviour is viewed.

It would seem, therefore, that today the female athlete is celebrated but traditional notions of gender are still influencing how she is viewed and indeed, how she might view herself. This gendering is manifested not only in the culture of sport as a masculine domain but in the predominance of a hegemonic femininity within women's sport that reinforces the archetypal view of women's physicality primarily as sexual. In addition, because our interpretations of gender appropriate behaviour are guided by our society's dominant ideology of heterosexuality (Butler, 1990) this sexuality is expected to be heterosexual. Thus, if the girl or woman wants to play the masculine game of sport she must do so in conformity with the patriarchal rules that ensure she is first and foremost recognised as a heterosexual feminine being.

Hegemonic femininity

The term hegemonic femininity is probably not as familiar to readers as the term hegemonic masculinity. Coined by sport scholars such as Lenskyj (1994) and Krane (1999), it is conceptualised as analogous, in the sports context, to hegemonic masculinity defined by Connell (1990) as 'the culturally idealised form of masculine character' (p. 83). Connell further contends that:

> To say that a particular form of masculinity is hegemonic means that it is culturally exalted and that its exaltation stabilizes a structure of dominance and oppression in the gender order as a whole.
>
> (Connell, 1990; p. 94)

In the world of women's sport, femininity can be seen to be exalted as hegemonic through the greater celebration of the 'feminine' female athlete. For example, female athletes who do not appear 'feminine' and/or who take part in sports perceived as male, or masculine, are likely to be treated more negatively by coaches and sport administrators, by competition judges and officials, by the media, by potential sponsors and by sports fans (Krane, 1999). Any of the above can ruin a woman's sporting career. Interview studies have shown that sportswomen are very aware of this and often go to great lengths to emphasise their femininity (e.g. Kolnes, 1995; Pirinen, 1997b; Krane et al, 1998). As Amy Acuff, US Olympic high jumper said in *Sports Illustrated for Women* magazine:

Too many people hold fast to the old image of female jocks. They have a problem with seeing female athletes as feminine and beautiful. Something unique has to be done to bring the public to the table. After that, they can see what great athletes we are.

(Layden, 1999; p. 111)

Acuff's 'something unique' was to compete in a fur trimmed bikini at a competition in February 1999, in a flesh coloured outfit that made her look naked from a distance at a competition in May 1999 and to pose nude with body paint for a Year 2000 calendar. Less 'unique' strategies are to wear make-up, hairstyles and clothing that emphasise a feminine appearance, to publicise the existence of a boyfriend/husband and children and to emphasise the 'we can be athletes and feminine too' theme (Krane, 1999). As coach Laurne Gregg says in an article about the US Women's National Soccer Team:

[They] are not afraid to be feminine. They have a wide range of interests outside of soccer, and some are even raising families. Plus, they're attractive.

(Hirshey, 1998; p. 99)

The question begging to be asked is why it is deemed so important for female athletes to be seen as feminine and beautiful? After all, we do not question whether male athletes are masculine and handsome. What emerges in this book is the importance of *visible* differences between women and men in our society. Bodily differences between men and women mean visible differences between masculinity and femininity. Bodies are most apparent in the context of sport and exercise because these are activities that usually involve some degree of undress in order to facilitate movement. Because the visibility of a woman with muscles, demonstrating strength, speed and agility is more consistent with traditional notions of masculinity, we need to be assured of the sportswoman's femininity, hence the emphasis on beauty and heterosexual desirability. This is deemed necessary both in the world of women's sport and in recreational exercise in order to prevent a diminishing of the visible differences between the masculine and the feminine. As Gillett and White (1992) argue, male physicality in sport represents:

a subtle form of symbolic domination rather than overt physical control, which contributes to the reproduction and reinforcement of power relations inherent in the existing gender order.

(Gillett and White, 1992; p. 363)

Thus, a diminishing of visible differences weakens gender boundaries and the power that the masculine hegemony holds in a patriarchal society. This diminishment can be resisted through hegemonic femininity and the gender order of male domination and female oppression thus upheld.

Towards a psychology of the physically active woman

In writing this book I have endeavoured to contribute to the development of a psychology of the physically active woman by examining her experiences from feminist and gendered perspectives. Chapter 2 provides some historical background. Not intended as a complete history of women in sport, it is framed around the Olympic movement and charts women's limited entry into this most prestigious of sporting events right up to the present day. At the same time this chapter charts the science that was used to exclude her. This science has not been able to conclusively show that women have lesser physical ability and therefore continue to justify her exclusion from many events. However, what does continue to restrict her participation is the influence of hegemonic femininity on how women's sports are viewed and experienced. This argument is further elaborated in Chapter 3 by examining how sportswomen today are challenged to demonstrate their heterosexual femininity through their treatment by the media, sporting organisations, corporate sponsors, sports fans and indeed wider society. Chapter 4 discusses the sport of female bodybuilding because the controversies surrounding the female bodybuilder could be said to epitomise the wider controversies surrounding femininity and what it means to be a (physically active) woman. In addition to a woman resisting notions of traditional femininity we also see how she is required to comply with them. Furthermore, we see how, as more women participate in this sport and as they achieve greater muscularity, greater efforts are made to prevent a diminishing of visible differences; to correct the female bodybuilder to cultural norms. In a different way the same phenomenon occurs in the world of women's recreational physical exercise where exercise has become the latest commodity in the highly commercialised beauty culture and in Chapter 5 I argue that this beauty activity serves to perpetuate traditional notions of femininity. In Chapter 6 I have attempted to place all of the above within a theoretical framework for answering the question how does the sporty type as masculine influence women's self-perceptions and their subsequent sport/exercise choices. Finally, in Chapter 7, I illustrate some ways in which change can and is occurring that will facilitate more positive experiences for girls and women so that they will be encouraged to be physically active and thus enrich their lives.

I recognise that the theoretical perspectives (feminist and gendered) that I am proposing are just one possible framework for one question and that my story in this chapter, plus the others presented in the remainder of this book, do not represent all possible stories. There are many other questions and other stories. I also recognise that women's involvement in sport and recreational exercise is multifactorial and many more frameworks, models, questions and approaches are being, or will need to be considered. Indeed, just as there is not one script of femininity (Ussher, 1997) but several, a single psychology of the physically active woman may be insufficient and several psychologies warranted. One of the factors in this multifactorial picture is the different stages of sport/exercise involvement: adoption, maintenance, dropping out and restarting. This is well established in the exercise psychology literature but I propose that it now needs to be examined in more detail from feminist and gendered perspectives. There are different gendered, as well as other non-gendered, issues and questions for different activities at each stage that need to be addressed both together and separately.

I have also only talked generally about sport and exercise. The only specific activities that I have addressed are bodybuilding and aerobics. Obviously women participate in many other sports and physical activities and it is likely that the issues of femininity that I have raised will apply either more or less depending on the activity under discussion (as well as the woman in question). It is also likely that numerous other issues that I have not touched on will be relevant. Moreover, women's involvement in physical activity is sure to vary throughout the life cycle and this also needs to be considered in relation to their physical and mental health needs. How gendering affects a woman's activity choices when she is starting a new career, family or both, when her family leave home, when she becomes widowed, are also important life cycle questions.

With all that in mind, I offer this book as a new beginning to the development of a psychology (or psychologies) of the physically active woman from critical, feminist, woman centred and gendered perspectives. It is noteworthy that in writing this book I have drawn on far more scholarship from the disciplines of sociology, popular culture, women's studies and media studies than I have any other. Yet, the problem of how to increase physical activity amongst women (and men) is a problem for psychology too. Whilst exercise psychologists have, of course, been concerned with increasing physical activity amongst the general population (amongst other health and exercise issues) exercise psychology is a relatively new field of research. Within this body of research I could not find any answers to the specific questions I posed for this book because moves away from androcentric, or male centred science towards more woman centred (gynecentric) science have yet to take place in a significant way. It is my hope that this book will contribute to making this move happen so that psychology can have an even greater impact on health policy and practice and therefore on women's lives.

Notes

1 Thirty minutes of moderate physical activity is required on a daily basis in order to glean significant health benefits (US Surgeon General, 1996).
2 Why some men do not see themselves as the sporty type is also an interesting and important question but will not be addressed in this book, which is about women.

2

A HERSTORY OF SPORT

Every four years, athletes from all over the world participate in the most prestigious of international sports events – the Olympic Games – which, due to its high sociocultural profile, attracts vast audiences worldwide. Since the beginning of the modern Olympic movement right up to the present day the belief that men are more physically suited to sports has been used to justify women's exclusion. Until his death in 1937, Baron Pierre de Coubertin, founder of the modern Olympics, was opposed to women's participation because he considered it to be unnatural and unaesthetic (Hargreaves, 1994). He defined the Olympic Games as:

> the solemn and periodic exaltation of male athleticism with inter-nationalism as a base, loyalty as a means, art for its setting and female applause as reward.
>
> (Women's Sports Foundation, 1995)

It is not, therefore, surprising that in 1896 women were excluded from the first modern Olympic Games held in Athens. Four years later in Paris, twelve women competed in tennis and golf at the second Olympic Games, but without the official consent of the International Olympic Committee (IOC). In London 1908, 43 women competed in figure skating, tennis and archery. Swimming was introduced for women in 1912 and, by 1920, 60 women competed out of a total 2,692. In 1928, 32 years after the men, track and field events were introduced for women (coinciding with the retirement of de Coubertin from the presidency of the IOC).

The inclusion of the 800 metre track event for women in 1928 was highly controversial as this was considered to be an exceedingly long way for women to run (Welch and Costa, 1994). Claims were made by the media that a number of women collapsed at the finishing line from exhaustion. Although these allegations have been denied (the women who 'collapsed' chose to lie down (DeFrantz, 1993)) this women's event was withdrawn from future Olympic Games until 1960. DeFrantz (1993) makes the inter-esting observation that in a report of the 1904 men's 800 metre track event,

13

two men truly did collapse on the track, one had to be carried to his training quarters and stimulants had to be administered to revive the other. The IOC did not consider this reason to withdraw the men's event from future Olympic Games.

Doubts about women's ability to participate in endurance events remained long after the women's 800 metres was reinstated in 1960 (Welch and Costa, 1994). For example, in 1978 the all-male IOC decided not to include a women's 3,000 metre event in the 1980 Moscow Olympics because it was considered too strenuous (Women's Sports Foundation, 1995). It was not until 1984 that this event and the marathon were finally included and the 5,000 and 10,000 metres were included only as recently as the Seoul Olympics in 1988. Judo was not included for women until 1992 and until very recently sports such as ice-hockey, football, modern pentathlon, weightlifting, some track and field events and the 1,500 metres freestyle swim were also among the exclusions. This is even though women competed in these events at other competitions and hold world records or other accolades for them. However, the most recent Olympic Games in Sydney, 2000, saw a changed and exciting situation, with eight additional sports open to women: hammer throw, modern pentathlon, pole vault, tae kwon do, trampoline, triathlon, water polo and weightlifting. This brings the number of Olympic sports open to women to a total of 26. Now, only two sports that are open to men, remain to be open to women – boxing and wrestling.

Biology as destiny

It may seem intuitively logical to conclude that women are indeed less suited to sports due to lesser physical ability, firstly because men, in general, are taller and stronger and from an early age it has been observed that they can throw further than women, run faster and hit harder (Young, 1990); and secondly because women's role in reproduction is not generally considered conducive to such activities. However, whilst it is true that there are sex differences in physical abilities such as running, throwing, etc., it is also true that the research into sex differences has revealed more similarities than differences between the sexes (Duda, 1991). For example, on average men are taller than women but there is great variability within groups of men and women so that many men are shorter than many women and many women are taller than many men. This is because individual differences within groups account for a greater percentage of the variance than that of the differences between groups (Eagly, 1987; Hyde, 1981). Furthermore, there are women from different cultures who are generally taller than men from other cultures, so generalisations from one culture or point in time cannot necessarily be made to another.

It must also be acknowledged that now women are allowed to compete in sport, they are breaking athletic records that men previously held, which argues against the biological position that men are naturally more suited to sports. For example, the 1988 world records for the women's 800 and 1,500 freestyle swimming events would have been world records for the equivalent men's events in 1972 and Janet Evans' 1988 400 metre freestyle time was more than 2 seconds faster than Mark Spitz's 1968 world record. In 1988, Florence Griffith Joyner's 100 metre world record of 10.64 seconds was just 0.72 of a second slower than Carl Lewis's 1988 world record of 9.92 seconds. Also in 1988 Paula Newby-Fraser was the female winner of the Bud Light Ironman Triathlon World Championship. She completed this event, a 2.4 mile ocean swim, a 112 mile bike ride and a 26.2 mile marathon, in 9 hours, 1 minute and 1 second (Burton-Nelson, 1991). This time is faster than all of the men in every Ironman triathlon prior to 1984, yet the Olympic triathlon was only open to women for the first time in the Sydney 2000 games. Overall, Newby-Fraser finished 11th, just 12 seconds after the man who placed 10th, and 30 minutes 1 second after the male winner. Of her win, Newby-Fraser remarked: 'I never thought a woman could go this fast' (Burton-Nelson, 1991).

The realisation that women can go that fast has led to women making gains which suggest that they are catching up with men. For example, Guttman (1991) notes that in a selection of eight track events the average of men's times in 1927 was 21.35% faster than the women's but in 1977 it was only 10.64%. In the 100 metre sprint, between 1956 and 1985, the difference between the women and the men went from 11.4% to 8%. Indeed, in all track events, women's improvements have been much greater than men's (Guttman, 1991). The women's marathon, and other long distance events, are particularly noteworthy in this respect, leading to the viewpoint that women are better than men at endurance sports. One early notable athlete in this regard is the long distance swimmer Gertrude Ederle who, in 1926, became the first woman to swim across the English channel. Her time was almost 2 hours faster than the five men who had succeeded in this event before she did. In the marathon, during the 10 years between 1972 and 1982 women's times improved by 16.2%, with a number finishing first overall in several marathons, 50 mile, 100 mile and 24 hour runs. One notable sportswoman in this sphere is Natalie Cullimore who, in 1971, won a race of over 100 miles that none of the men finished (and it was not until 17 years later in Seoul, 1988, that women were allowed to compete in the Olympic marathon). These observations make it more likely that women's supposed inferior physical prowess is due to their having had less opportunity, resources and encouragement to develop these skills. Nonetheless, biological reductionism continues to be given credence and used to explain all kinds of behavioural differences between women and men (Fausto-Sterling, 1997; Nicolson, 1999; Choi, 1999a).

Protecting women as mothers

The most vociferous biological position which attempts to justify sport as the natural order of things for men but not for women is women's reproductive capacity. According to Leigh (1974; cited in DeFrantz, 1993), Baron de Coubertin believed that 'a woman's glory rightfully came through the number and quality of children she produced and that as far as sports were concerned, her greatest accomplishment was to encourage her sons to excel rather than to seek records for herself'. For centuries in almost all societies such attitudes have been put forward as a justification for excluding women not just from sport, but also from education and the workforce (Ussher, 1989) and continues today to such an extent in Western societies that the menstrual cycle, pregnancy and menopause are treated as illnesses (Gannon, 1998). The proposed danger is that energy spent on these activities might diminish the woman's reproductive power and result in fewer babies being born (e.g. Maudsley, 1874; Spencer, 1896).

This fear has not been upheld by the research findings. In young athletes menarche can be delayed and in athletes who train very intensively and/or participate in sports where low levels of body fat result (e.g. long distance running) or are required (e.g. gymnastics), menstrual irregularities can occur such as amenorrhoea (absence of menses) or oligomenorrhoea (scanty or infrequent menstruation). These irregularities are thought to be caused by low levels of body fat, which affects oestrogen levels, but once the intensive training lessens, body fat increases and menstrual function returns to normal (Prior, 1992). There is no evidence of damage to reproductive function in later life although there is some concern about bone density. As low oestrogen levels cause reductions in bone density, the athlete is at greater risk of fractures (DeSouza et al, 1994). However, in the recreational exercisers, the opposite is true as numerous studies have found that physical exercise *increases* bone density (Gannon, 1999). The risk of osteoporosis in later life is, therefore, reduced if a woman has exercised regularly during her younger years.

Thus, the scientific research indicates that there does not appear to be any danger to women's reproductive health from vigorous exercise (just as there is none from education or employment). If and when adverse changes occur, they are temporary and reversible and tend to be restricted to a particular group of athletes. As a result, Prior (1992) questions the predominant disease model of sportswomen's menstrual function as this reinforces the false notion that any changes are indicative of disease that requires treatment. She suggests that the changes be considered as the body's ability to adapt to physical demands. This adaptation model is a more positive construction of reproductive change and takes into account the various other factors, such as nutrition and psychological stress, that also have an influence on the menstrual cycle (Walker, 1997).

Not only have female athletes successfully borne healthy babies, they have also continued to train and compete during pregnancy. For example, in 1948, a Dutch sprinter, Fanny Blankerskoen, won four Olympic gold medals. At the time, she was 3 months pregnant with her third child. In 1989 the late British mountaineer Alison Hargreaves was pregnant when she became the first British woman to climb the 5,000 feet North Wall of the Eiger in the Swiss Alps. More recent examples include Alex Powe-Allred who, at the 1994 tryouts for the US women's bobsled team, was 4 months pregnant with her second child (Powe-Allred and Powe, 1997). Bobsled competitors are required to push a 325 lb sled for 50 metres and at these try-outs, the eight fastest women qualified for the team. Not only did Powe-Allred make the team, she was also the fastest competitor. The woman who was placed second, Liz Parr-Smestad, was 3 months pregnant with her first child (Powe-Allred and Powe, 1997). Ultramarathoner Sue Olsen competed in a 24 hour race in 1995 and gave birth 30 hours later.

In addition to continuing to train and compete during pregnancy, female athletes often return to training very soon after childbirth. US diver Pat McCormick competed in the 1956 Olympic Games 5 months after having a baby, winning gold in both the springboard and the platform dive events. This made her the first person, male or female, to win both events. Distance runner Gwyn Coogan began running 2 weeks after the birth of her daughter in 1993 and 10 weeks later she qualified for the US cross-country team. Sky, one of the stars of the American TV show The Gladiators, was in the gym leg pressing 1,000 lb when she went into labour with her second baby. She had the baby on Friday and was back in the gym on Monday.

Given the *lack* of evidence suggesting that our elite female athletes have diminished reproductive power, it should be clear that there is no reproductive danger to recreational exercisers. However, in a recent edition of the prestigious *New England Journal of Medicine* (NEJM), the first paragraph of an editorial on women and exercise cautions women against exercising intensely and for long periods of time as it 'may lead to menstrual and reproductive dysfunction' (Manson and Min-Lee, 1996; p. 1325). The evidence that they refer to is that which I have referred to above which (a) shows that any reproductive changes that might occur are temporary and (b) is relevant to a particular group of elite athletes only. Recreational exercisers do not train at the same intensity levels as elite athletes so warning them of the dangers for elite sportswomen is unjustified. Yet, the authors advocate moderate intensity exercise, such as brisk walking for 30 minutes, as it has fewer health risks than vigorous activity and go on to say:

We do not mean to discount the additional health benefits that may accrue with more frequent, longer and more intense physical activity, and we would not dissuade those who wish to exercise more. We do believe, however, that at some point the risks outweigh the health benefits of physical activity. If amenorrhea, reproductive disorders or repeated musculoskeletal injuries occur, we believe that the level of exercise that produces these complications is excessive, regardless of its health benefits.

(Manson and Min-Lee, 1996; p. 1326)

This is certainly true but the level at which exercise becomes excessive enough to cause reproductive change is way beyond the capabilities (and possibly interests) of the average person. It is a big jump from encouraging a sedentary American population to walk briskly every day to warning them of the dangers of exercising at the level of the elite athlete. Furthermore, overtraining can certainly cause changes to reproductive function but this can occur in both women and men[1] (Prior, 1992; Cumming, 1992). However, sportsmen's reproductive dysfunction receives far less discussion (Vertinsky, 1997), masking men's vulnerability and thereby giving the impression, as the NEJM article does, that this is a problem for women only. Moreover, this continual highlighting of women's reproductive capacity reiterates to women that their fertility is of primary concern and that they might endanger their chances of reproducing by exercising too much. Not only is the latter unsubstantiated empirically, evidence indicates recreational physical exercise to be beneficial to women's reproductive health (Mutrie and Choi, 2001). We reached this conclusion from our review (Choi and Mutrie, 1997) where we report that high levels (three or more times a week) of physical activity are associated with less negative mood premenstrually; women who continue to be physically active during pregnancy report more positive body image; and both pre- and post-menopause, women who engage in physical activity report increased psychological well-being and self-esteem compared to those who do not. This is not discussed in the NEJM article and the cautioning tone suggests that a desire to uphold the view of women as the physically inferior sex is more prevalent than objective, unequivocal scientific truth.

This discourse is not a new one as a disease model of women's reproduction has been evident since the Victorian era (Ussher, 1991). Beginning with the womb that was incorrectly thought to wander around the body making women hysterical and culminating today in raging hormones that are assumed to cause premenstrual syndrome, post-natal depression and menopause syndrome (in spite of evidence to the contrary[2]), women remain controlled through reproduction. As the definition of the healthy woman remains the woman able and willing to bear children, if she does not conform to this definition she is deemed to have an illness that requires treatment (Gannon, 1998). Hence the predominance of the disease model of sportswomen's menstrual function as opposed to Prior's adaptation model mentioned earlier. A positive construction of reproductive change would not provide an argument for limiting women's participation in sport.

Questioning biological femaleness

Is it a coincidence, therefore, that the introduction of sex testing came with the increased participation of women in the Olympic Games of the 1960s and 1970s and that only sports*women* are required to undergo this test? So strong is the belief that superior athletic prowess is the *natural* domain of men that women whose sporting performance is superior to men's cannot truly be women or are assumed to be men in disguise (Birrell and Cole, 1994). Indeed, two recent events that were brought to my attention illustrate this very well. The first is the case of a very talented young girl who was allowed to play on her school's (boy's) soccer team who one day played so well that the parent of one of the boys on the opposing team demanded to see her genitals as proof that she was a girl. The second is the 1999 World Veterans Athletics Games where American athlete Kathy Jaeger broke the 100 metre world record. She had to undergo a sex test because other competitors complained that she was too good to be a woman (Smith, 1999).

The stated rationale for sex testing is to prevent men from illegally entering women's events (IOC, 1992) but women who competed in events where the sexes were not segregated (e.g. trap shooting) were still tested and the IOC have never provided a justification for this (Wackwitz, 1996). Moreover, there has only ever been one case of a man masquerading as a woman in sporting events – a German athlete in the 1930s who did so at the request of the Nazi Youth Movement (Ewing, 1992; the reason for this request was not reported). In the case of the male to female transsexual tennis player Renee Richards (see below), she was not found to have any advantage over her female competitors (Birrell and Cole, 1994). The sex test, therefore, proves to the Olympic official that the athlete is not a man and proves to the athlete that she is indeed a woman (Wackwitz, 1996). This was significant to one long distance runner in 1968 who, according to Wackwitz (1996), was worried that she was indeed male because she ran so well she could outrun most of her female contemporaries. When she passed the test, she was 'elated'.

Initially (1966–1968) the sex test consisted of posing nude in front of a panel of judges for a visual examination of genitalia (Ljungqvist and Simpson, 1992). Although the genitalia were meant to be the focus of the examination, it is reported that comments about the sportswomen's chests were often made by the examiners, with flat chested athletes being treated with greater insensitivity (Lenskyj, 1986). The chief sex tester at the 1968 Olympics is said to have told reporters that from his examination of 911 female athletes he concluded that sports made them ugly with unattractive bodies and in some cases, hair on their chests (Lenskyj, 1986). As Lenskyj points out, the sex testers appeared to have difficulty distinguishing between biological femaleness and sex appeal.

Later the visual test was replaced by a more technologically advanced test where cells taken from the inside of the woman's cheek were subjected to genetic analysis (Ljungqvist and Simpson, 1992). If the woman was found not to have two complete X chromosomes or to have a Y chromosome, she was disqualified from the Olympics and barred from future competition for life. A number of female athletes have been found to have genetic abnormalities which they did not know about and have subsequently been barred from performance, sometimes with much media vilification. Many of these have been wrongly eliminated as their genetic disorders do not give them any physical advantage over other female competitors (Hall, 1996). This reduction of the evaluation of biological femaleness to a single criterion which biomedical science alone was empowered to decide is problematic for a number of reasons, not least because about 10% of the population are not either XX-female or XY-male due to chromosomal anomalies which can take many forms such as XXY-females or XX-males. Therefore, as Birrell and Cole (1994) point out in relation to transsexualism, which is equally applicable to the chromatin sex test, what is a 'woman' and how has she been constructed? By chromosomes alone? They also ask on what basis should the decision be made? Usually, sex is determined at birth by visual examination of the external genitalia but transsexualism indicates that this is not always sufficient, as do women with androgen insensitivity syndrome (AIS). The latter are XY but, due to either complete or partial insensitivity to androgens, are born with ambiguous external genitalia and subsequently diagnosed as female. Butler points out that 'gendered meanings frame the hypothesis and the reasoning of those biomedical inquiries that seek to establish "sex" for us as it is prior to the cultural meanings that it acquires' (Butler, 1990; p. 109). Thus, the decision that 'woman' is signified by an XX individual, or a vagina, or both, is a cultural convention. As a result, Lorber argues that although bodies may differ physiologically in a variety of ways, 'they are completely transformed by social practices to fit into the salient categories of a society, the most pervasive of which are "female" and "male" and "women" and "men"' (Lorber, 1993; p. 569). For women with AIS, therefore, the problems that they encounter as a result of their condition, are not due to their biology but to a society which does not know what to do with someone who does not fall neatly into one of the two accepted categories (Kitzinger, 2000).

A further example of the sociocultural nature of sex determination can be seen in the case of the transsexual Renee Richards and her fight to play women's tennis. It is also indicative of how sex testing in sport is about addressing disparities between beliefs about, and expectations of, the feminine woman and her athletic performance through biological reductionism. When she announced her intention to compete in the US Women's Open Singles tournament it was made a requirement by the governing bodies that all competitors undergo a sex chromatin test. Richards refused and was not allowed to participate. She then took her case to the New York Supreme Court who ruled in her favour on the grounds that she was now a woman and that the sex test was discriminatory and a violation of her human rights. The United States Tennis Association was intent on appealing this decision but later changed its mind. Initially, opposition from the tennis world to Richards' participation was framed around protecting women tennis players from the advantages she was assumed to have solely by having been born with a male body. It was also feared that Richards would set a precedent for other males to become transsexuals in order to compete against women and win (Kane, 1995). These arguments could only be put forward on the grounds that women's bodies were physically inferior and the years of privileged access to sport which Richards enjoyed when she was a man were never considered in the public debates that ensued (Birrell and Cole, 1994). However, her performance in the 1977 US Open was poor and this was the basis upon which she was finally accepted as a woman by the tennis world. The United States Tennis Association verified this when it decided not to appeal the ruling of the Supreme Court (Birrell and Cole, 1994). Richards is reported as saying in *The New York Times*, 18 August 1976, that her poor performance 'served to inform the public that I was not an unbeatable behemoth out to prey on helpless little girls' (Birrell and Cole, 1994). It is noteworthy that 3 years earlier one of these helpless little girls, Billie Jean King, tennis champion and campaigner for equal rights for sportswomen, challenged former male Wimbledon tennis champion Bobby Riggs to a tennis match which she won. Nonetheless, Richards' poor performance at women's tennis seemed to provide 'proof' that she was indeed a woman even though she would fail a chromatin sex test.

Over the years since the inception of sex testing, many medical bodies, such as the American Medical Association and the American College of Obstetrics and Gynecology, have denied the need and scientific rationale for sex testing. The particular genetic test used has been criticised as unreliable as it yields both false positive and false negative results. Many consider the notion of sex testing to be degrading and discriminatory against women as well as a waste of time and money, but the IOC still insist on the need to expose the man masquerading as woman. Many other sporting bodies do not enforce the IOC policy. Indeed some are vigorously opposed to it on the grounds that it is unethical and humiliating to women to question their existence as females and their prowess as athletes (Ljungqvist and Simpson, 1992), but since its inception the IOC have denied charges that sex testing is an infringement of human rights. In 1992 the International Amateur Athletic Federation abolished sex testing completely and introduced a medical examination for all athletes (male and female) that would include a visual inspection of the genitalia. But sadly, the traditional method of testing is still required by most international sports federations.

Feminine appropriate sports

When the IOC began to introduce women's events into the programme they would only allow a small number of 'feminine appropriate' ones (Welch and Costa, 1994). In 1912 this was swimming, tennis, figure-skating and archery and as described earlier, many exclusions remained over the years despite the fact that women competed in these events at other competitions. One has to ask, what are the criteria that determine the feminine appropriateness of a sport? This is difficult to determine, however, as the rules governing the sports programme make no mention of either feminine or masculine appropriateness. The Olympic Charter lists only the following criteria for inclusion:

> Only sports widely practised by men in at least seventy-five countries and on four continents, and by women in at least forty countries and on three continents, may be included in the programme of the Games of the Olympiad. (For the winter games it is twenty-five countries and three continents with no sex differentiation.)
> (The Olympic Charter, III, 5.2.1, www.olympic.org)

Thus, judgements about feminine appropriateness can only be based on subjective criteria derived from personal attitudes and beliefs. Indeed, in the above objective criteria there is still an element of subjectivity. Women wrestle and box in more than three continents of the world but how many participants are required for a sport to be considered 'widely practised' enough to be included? The answer to this question is not contained within the rules as listed on the Olympic web site.

The answer is also not contained in the scientific research as it merely documents the belief that certain activities are acceptable for females and others are not. For example, Colley et al (1987) found that from a list of 50 sports or physical activities, 24 of them were not considered suitable for females (classified as suitable for males only) by a group of 291 British 16 to 18 year olds. These included aggressive and competitive sports such as boxing, rugby and wrestling, as well as risk taking sports such as mountaineering, potholing and hang-gliding. Only five were considered unsuitable for males, i.e. for females only: netball, yoga, popmobility (nowadays known as aerobics or exercise to music), lacrosse and rounders. The authors also asked what sports were considered suitable for both sexes but did not report what these were. They did report the interesting finding that more male than female participants gender-typed sports.

In a similar study using American undergraduates, Csizma et al (1988) asked participants to rate 68 sports and physical activities on a scale of 1 (strongly masculine) to 7 (strongly feminine). Twelve were considered feminine and included four kinds of dance, two kinds of skating, field hockey, gymnastics and yoga. In contrast 30 were considered masculine and these included boxing, football, rugby and weightlifting. The remaining 26 were considered neutral (e.g. handball, backpacking, sailing, swimming and running). Csizma et al (1988) also asked a second sample of undergraduates to rate the social acceptability of males and females to participate in each sport and the likelihood that they would do so. Not surprisingly the acceptability and likelihood of participation in masculine sports was greater for males than for females and the acceptability and likelihood of participation in feminine sports was greater for females than for males. For the neutral sports, the findings for male and female participants were similar.

Interesting though these findings are they do not tell us why the research participants rated certain activities more appropriate for males than for females. That is, what is it about the activity and/or about women and men that determines this? From the earlier Olympic exclusions, particularly long distance events, one might deduce that beliefs about women's physical inferiority were once influential. Given the 2000 Olympics, it seems that women's physical ability is now less of an issue, but if we look a little deeper it can be seen that this is not necessarily the case. In looking at sports where women have participated for some time, we see some where they can only participate in the female versions. These ensure that the participants cannot be considered masculine and their appearance masks the physical strength required by the athlete from the viewer.

For example, in gymnastics some of the events are different for women and men in order to emphasise harmony and rhythm (femininity) in women but strength and power (masculinity) in men (Pfister, 1998). Thus, only women take part in events such as the balance beam and rhythmic gymnastics (dance like floor movements with a long ribbon). In the floor work section, which both women and men take part in, the women do so with musical accompaniment and the men without. Presumably this is because looking pretty whilst dancing to music with a long ribbon is not considered a masculine appropriate activity, just as synchronised swimming, an event open only to women, is not. Furthermore, the young, small and light female gymnast has become representative of the genuinely feminine gymnast (Pfister, 1998). Lorber argues that gymnastics for females are actually girls' gymnastics – 'slim, wiry, prepubescent girls and not mature women . . . little girls who will be disqualified as soon as they grow up' (Lorber, 1993; p. 571). Male gymnasts, on the other hand, are grown up, muscular and mature (Lorber, 1993).

More recent research suggests that gender-stereotyped beliefs about sport might be changing in the younger generation. A study of British secondary school children found no interactions between sex and sport and no evidence that female sports participants were viewed more negatively than males (Howat et al, 1994). Whilst these findings suggest optimism for the future, the authors warn that they may be a result of children's increasing awareness of political correctness which determined their responses, rather than any real change in beliefs (Howat et al, 1994). Children certainly are more 'politically correct', as Williams and Bedward (1999) discovered when they asked school children if they felt that particular activities were for girls or boys only. Almost all responded that such views were sexist. However, girls' experiences of mixed sex soccer teams in the USA (see Chapter 6, this volume) certainly indicate that beliefs have not changed significantly. Furthermore, children continue to report beliefs consistent with the stereotypes in relation to playing musical instruments, which is another activity that is gendered. O'Neill and Boulton (1996) and Harrison and O'Neill (2000) found this in 9–11 year old and 7–8 year old children respectively. In both these studies, both boys and girls were very clear that instruments such as flute and piano were more appropriate for girls to play and instruments such as brass and drums more appropriate for boys. These studies suggest that, in music at least, attitudes are not changing.

Fighting women

The continued exclusion of women's boxing and wrestling from the Olympic Games might be suggestive that attitudes are also not changing in sport. Over the last few years a number of events and rulings concerning women's boxing in Britain have generated much publicity which is somewhat revealing in terms of attitudes towards fighting women. In November 1996 the Amateur Boxing Association of England announced that females over 10 years old would be allowed to box competitively in Britain from October 1997. Both supporters and non-supporters of men's boxing were horrified (Greer, 1999), indicating that for girls and women to fight and be physically violent is not considered feminine appropriate behaviour. Perhaps it is not surprising then that in 1998, Jane Couch, women's world welterweight boxing champion, was refused a licence to box professionally by the British Boxing Board of Control (BBBC). The reasons for refusal were risks to an unborn child, menstrual pain and that premenstrual women were more accident and injury prone and more emotionally unstable (de Bertodano, 1998). Couch claimed sex discrimination and an industrial tribunal ruled in her favour in March 1998. She can now box professionally in Britain and her first fight in London the following November (prior to her British licence Couch's fights had to be held overseas, usually in the USA) was boycotted by a number of boxing officials (Women's Boxing Page, 1999). British boxing promoter Frank Maloney is reported by *The Daily Telegraph* newspaper as saying: 'In my opinion all officials should have boycotted it, and I take my hat off to those officials of the British Boxing Board of Control who declined to work the show' (Women's Boxing Page, 1999). He is also reported as having told the BBC that women only belong in the boxing ring as ring card girls (Women's Boxing Page, 1999). Ring card girls appear in between rounds dressed in bikinis and walk seductively around the ring holding a card above their heads announcing the round number. They are usually received with much leering and whistling from the men.

Henry Cooper, a former British champion boxer turned sports commentator, during a recent radio news report proclaimed that 'girls' fighting was not 'nice' and that parents would not want their daughters coming home with broken noses and black eyes. This seems to imply that they would not mind this happening to their sons and that fighting boys are okay, presumably because this is masculine appropriate. In a similar vein, Maloney's comment above seems to imply that it is more feminine appropriate for girls and women to provide sexual entertainment for men. Indeed, women boxers and wrestlers have been ridiculed through references to mud wrestling and other forms of sexual entertainment (Krane, 1999). In a study of 12 professional female boxers in the USA, Halbert found that the women experienced a 'dualism of women boxers as sexual object and women boxers who challenge traditional femininity' (Halbert, 1997; p. 17). This was manifested in assumptions that the woman was either a 'Foxee' boxer (sexual entertainer) or a lesbian and were prevalent amongst male boxers in the gym as well as amongst trainers, boxing promoters and officials.

In short, these arguments against women's boxing are concerned with women looking 'nice' and suitably feminine – that is, not physically violent. In focussing on this some very important facts are ignored. Firstly, women are not simply all sugar and spice – that they can be aggressive and violent when they want to be. Secondly, there is no reproductive or hormonal basis for not allowing women to box. The research evidence shows that they are not significantly more violent, more accident prone, more emotionally unstable, or more anything, during particular phases of their menstrual cycle. In terms of risks to an unborn child, this can be avoided by requiring the woman to take a pregnancy test before her boxing match. Thirdly, attention is deflected away from the very important fact that we do not know if there are additional medical risks for women due to lack of research. Fourthly, they ignore the medical effects that are the same as those for male boxers, such as the risk of brain damage. The day before the decision not to grant Couch a licence was publicised the life support machine of a male boxer, brain dead due to a lethal punch to the head, had been turned off (Greer, 1999). And finally, as with the non-discussion of the effects of overtraining on men's reproductive health, this non-discussion of effects on men serves to hide men's vulnerability. It also reveals how aware the (male) boxing establishment is of the effects that injury to women could have on public opinion of men's boxing and how tenuous the idea of male invincibility is. Boxing promoter Frank Warren comments that he would not promote Jane Couch even though 'she boxes well for a woman' (de Bertodano, 1998). He is against women boxing because 'If there was a tragedy and a woman was carried out of the ring on a stretcher, I don't feel there would be any support for the sport' (de Bertodano, 1998). Medical opinion is also consistent with this view as Bennett (1998) reports that Adrian Whiteson, the medical adviser to the BBBC, in giving evidence to the industrial tribunal hearing Couch's case remarks:

> I have no objections to women boxing . . . However, boxing is a high-risk sport which can cause injury and death which causes public concern. Should such a tragedy occur when a woman is boxing the whole sport would suffer such adverse publicity that the continuation of the sport would be at risk.
>
> (Bennett, 1998)

When asked by de Bertodano why it is worse if a woman gets killed, Warren's response was 'It's the same thing as women in the front line of a war. If women soldiers started getting killed I don't think that would sit too well with the general public' (de Bertodano, 1998). Thus, men fighting and killing each other, inside or outside of a boxing ring, is acceptable but women doing so, is not.

Questioning femininity

Behaving in a manner deemed not feminine appropriate may lead to the girl's or woman's femininity being questioned. This can be seen in the way that girls who like to climb trees and play sports are dubbed tomboys (Money and Ehrhardt, 1972) – boys who *do not* are dubbed cissies, and sportswomen are dubbed lesbians (Krane, 1996; Chapter 3, this volume). The 1970s and 1980s saw considerable research by social scientists into female athletes and their gender orientation. This research stemmed from social psychological theories of gender orientation, such as those of Bem (1974) and Spence et al (1975), whose constructs and psychometric measures of masculinity, femininity and androgyny, were applied to the female athlete to investigate this question of their gender. In the case of Bem, a sex role inventory containing 20 stereotypically feminine items (e.g. affectionate, sensitive to the needs of others), 20 stereotypically masculine items (e.g. independent, willing to take risks) and 20 filler items (e.g. happy, truthful) was developed. An androgyny score was calculated based on the difference between the feminine and masculine scores. In the case of Spence, the Personality Attributes Questionnaire (PAQ), developed simultaneously, was of a similar format but measured masculinity and femininity only. Thus, during the 1970s and 1980s a wealth of research using Bem's Sex Role Inventory (BSRI) and Spence et al's PAQ found that female athletes scored higher on the constructs of androgyny or masculinity than female non-athletes (Gill, 1994). Interestingly, this has also been found to be the case for female scientists (Helmreich and Spence, 1977).

These are not really surprising findings. Sport, like science and other male dominated occupations, is highly competitive and individuals, both male and female, need to be competitive, instrumental, assertive, independent and willing to take risks in order to succeed. Competition and aggression, in particular, are prevalent in sport so of course sportswomen will score highly on these terms but this does not mean that sportswomen are less feminine or more masculine. What it does mean is that the social construction of masculinity deems these attributes to be masculine and that in compiling the measurement scales, this has influenced the researchers in their labelling of characteristics as either masculine or feminine. Conducting this kind of research shows such qualities to be considered more desirable for males than females (otherwise why would the sportswoman's femininity be questioned?) and that these questionnaires are merely demonstrating how gender is constructed as opposed to any real personality or individual differences. This has been recognised in the critiques of the gender orientation theories that have come about alongside the growing awareness of the social construction of gender and the 1990s have seen less use of tools such as the BSRI and the PAQ in research. Perhaps this is also a reflection of changes in the attitudes of the researchers and the 1990s social concept of political correctness.

The 'masculine' girl

It is not only psychological science that has been used to question the femininity of the physically active woman in the 1970s. Biological science rears its head again in its assumption that she is more masculine than non-active females and the hormone testosterone has been the variable of investigation. This is because testosterone is a sex hormone present in both males and females but males have higher levels. It is known that testosterone is responsible for masculinising the foetus in the womb and for the physical changes experienced by males at puberty. It is also thought to play a role in aggression and sexual behaviour due to findings from research on non-human animals, such as rats (Carlson, 1995). What effects prenatal over-exposure to testosterone might have on humans has been investigated by assessing girls who are born with a condition known as female pseudohermaphroditism which can result from a genetic disorder that causes the adrenal glands to produce too much androgen (known as androgenital syndrome (AGS)). The female foetus, therefore, becomes masculinised. She is born with a uterus, fallopian tubes and ovaries but her clitoris and labia are abnormal. Female pseudohermaphroditism can also occur as a result of drugs that induce high levels of androgens in the pregnant woman's circulation. From a study of 10 girls whose mothers had received progestins during pregnancy, a treatment that masculinised the external genitalia of otherwise normal XX girls, and 15 AGS girls, Money and Ehrhardt (1972) reported that these girls were more tomboyish (their definition included a preference for vigorous athletic activity, especially outdoor pursuits) than normal controls, preferred toy cars and guns to dolls and considered career more important than marriage. Aggressive behaviour was not affected. From these results they concluded that over-exposure to prenatal androgens masculinised the girls' brains, subsequently causing them to behave in a masculine way.

A further study was conducted to improve on the experimental design of the previous study (Ehrhardt and Baker, 1978). In the previous study the normal controls were not related to the AGS girls but in the new study the control group was made up of family members. In addition, another control group of boys with AGS was included. The findings were similar to the previous study. The AGS girls were considered to be more physically active than their unaffected sisters but there was no difference in aggressive behaviour. AGS boys were also more physically active but not more aggressive than their unaffected brothers.

These two studies are so methodologically flawed, however, that it cannot be concluded that over-exposure to prenatal androgens causes girls to be more masculine. First, in some cases the girls were taking drug treatment to correct their condition and how this might have affected their behaviour was not considered. Second, all of the girls had received corrective surgery (i.e. circumcision) for their condition and again, how this might affect their behaviour was not considered – there is some evidence that suggests sex differences are related to circumcision (Richards et al, 1976). Third, data collection was not rigorous. It was the children themselves and their family members who rated the child's behaviour and not independent observers who were unaware of which children had AGS. Observer bias may, therefore, have occurred. Fourth, alternative interpretations of their data should be considered, not least because of the strong evidence that shows behaviour to be influenced by environment (e.g. the different ways boys and girls are treated as discussed in Chapter 1). In a later review of these and other studies into the effect of prenatal hormones on aggression, Meyer-Bahlburg and Ehrhardt (1982) acknowledged some of these criticisms, but still maintained that sex differences in aggression have a biological basis. We do not know yet whether this is the case or not. The authors' argument might be strengthened if all, or at least many, female athletes had been over-exposed to androgens prenatally but, as far as I am aware, there is no evidence to suggest this. In her review of the literature on children who have been over-exposed to masculinising hormones and children who have been over-exposed to feminising hormones, Fausto-Sterling concludes that 'not a single one of these studies is unequivocal. Several contradict each other, while the number of uncontrolled variables makes it impossible to interpret. The claim that clear-cut evidence exists to show that fetal hormones make boys more active, aggressive or athletic than girls is little more than fancy, although harmless it is not' (Fausto-Sterling, 1994; p. 141). Similar conclusions were reached by Hall (1996) and, as this type of research continues to flourish[3] in spite of the methodological critiques, she suggests that science is determined to perpetuate the myth that the physically active female is in some way deviant. I have argued elsewhere (Choi, 1999a) that within the sports and biomedical sciences good science has prevailed far less than androcentric bias in order to uphold the view of male superiority and female inferiority. There appears to be a need to do this to maintain the patriarchal hegemony because, as Duncan (1990) notes, sport is one of the last masculine strong-holds where men have been able to demonstrate their superiority over women. Sport is about physical activity and is therefore a way through which biological or physical differences can interface with the social con-structions of gender (Kane and Greendorfer, 1994). By its very nature sport provides opportunities to demonstrate male superiority in strength, muscu-larity and physicality which can then be equated with social power. This cannot be more apparent than in the example of women boxers sparring with male boxers. Sparring sessions simulate a real fight in order to enable the fighters to practise their skills on a real opponent in a safe and controlled manner. The objective is not to injure or knock them out (as it is in a real fight) so protective headgear is worn and the exercise is controlled. Due to the lack of female boxers in the gym, the women inevitably have to spar with a man, leading to direct confrontation with their negative attitudes:

> You know, whenever two guys that go in the ring, of course they mess around with each other. You know, and kind of respect each other. Of course you go in there to fight, right, but the guys aren't gonna go in there to kill each other. But whenever they got in there to fight with me, their intentions was to get me out of there. So I got some beatings. I've had my share of beatings from the guys.
>
> (Halbert, 1997; p. 20)

The potential danger in this situation was described by another boxer:

> But when you spar with these guys, you can kind of feel that you're not really wanted there. You can feel their punches. Especially if you hit them, oh boy, they're going to come back at you . . . They lose total control. I mean, they just . . . their male ego gets hurt, I guess. 'There's no way this woman's gonna hit me.' Many a times they come at me, and I give it to them too.
>
> (Halbert, 1997; p. 21)

In her book *The stronger women get, the more men love football*, Mariah Burton-Nelson (1994), sports writer and former professional basketball player, describes sport as 'one of the few remaining endeavours where male muscle matters' (p. 6) and 'as women in the late twentieth century gain

3

THE SPORTING WOMAN

Given the threat of the female athlete to the masculine domain of sport, it is perhaps not surprising that sportswomen soon learn that they, and their achievements, are less important than men's. One way that this occurs is through the lesser recognition that female athletes receive in the media and the kind of representations of sportswomen that are portrayed. Men's sport receives far more media coverage than women's and when women's sport is covered it is often trivialised, marginalised and sexualised (Cohen, 1993). Research reported by the Sports Council (1993) found that only 0.5–5% of total sports space in British national newspapers is devoted to women's sport. Theberge (1991a), in an analysis of sports coverage in Canadian newspapers, found only 2.3–14.4% to be afforded to women's sport. A study in Australia reported only 1.3% of sports coverage being female (McKay and Rowe, 1987) and in Germany, 4.3–6.75% has been reported (Klein, 1988). Magazines are similarly lacking, with only 9% of 3,723 articles in the American *Sports Illustrated* being found to feature sportswomen and black sportswomen receiving even less coverage than white sportswomen and black sportsmen (Lumpkin and Williams, 1991). However, figures for the 1990s appear to show a slight improvement. In the USA they now range from 3.25% to 25% and in Australia from 1.3% to 4.5%, although these findings must be viewed with caution as research methods between studies vary enormously (Matheson and Flatten, 1996).

Unfortunately, British coverage does not appear to be improving. Figures released by the Women's Sports Foundation (WSF) in 1998[1] show coverage still at 5% and an unpublished study conducted in 1998 by Tamsin Mason[2] found coverage in *The Times* (a broadsheet) to be 11.5% over a 3 month period; 0.5% in *The Sun* (a tabloid) also over a 3 month period and 7–8% in the two sports magazines that she assessed between October 1997 and May 1998.

As the number of women participating in sport is increasing, one might expect to find a proportional increase in reporting but Matheson and Flatten (1996) have not found this to be the case and in a study of British print media they actually found a decrease. Based on a 7% increase in the proportion of women athletes from Britain participating in the Olympic Games between 1984 (32%) and 1992 (39%; Sports Council, 1993) Matheson and Flatten (1996) hypothesised a similar increase in female sport coverage. Six British national daily and Sunday newspapers from the same two weeks in July of 1984 and 1994 were examined. Comparisons were made on number of front page articles, total number of articles, number of front page photographs, total number of photographs and square centimetres of text. They found that number of articles per day decreased by 6%, number of square centimetres decreased by 10% and number of photographs decreased by 14%. The British print media clearly need enlightening! In an attempt to do this the UK Sports Council, in July 1995, produced the *Women and the Sports Media UK Directory and Media Guide* for wide distribution. Its aims were to provide guidelines for journalists on the coverage of women's sport and to increase the numbers of women working in the media by providing a directory of women working in different aspects of the sports media. Based on the findings presented here it would appear that little change has been effected by this excellent publication and in spite of an increase in female sports journalists.

Of course when coverage is part of a prestigious international sporting event the figures are higher but still much smaller then those for men. For example, analysis of British coverage of the 1991 World Athletic Championships and the 1992 Olympic Games found that around a quarter of total coverage was devoted to women (Alexander, 1994). This study examined articles from seven daily and Sunday newspapers for the period of these sporting events. Alexander (1994) measured the number of headlines, number of written lines, number of photographs and size of photographic area and for all four, in both events, sportsmen received three times more coverage than sportswomen. These findings cannot be explained by the fact that more male athletes competed than female or that more male athletes achieved success because the amount of coverage received was not in proportion. Alexander (1994) also points out that in cases where a female athlete attained comparable success, such as the 1991 World Athletics Championships 800 metres hurdles where Sally Gunnell won the women's event and Roger Black won the men's, Gunnell did not attract similar levels of coverage to Black. Similarly, at the 1992 Olympic Games, when both Sally Gunnell and Linford Christie won gold medals for Britain, Alexander's (1994) study showed that 59 photographs were of Christie and 36 of Gunnell. Similar findings have also been reported in studies of Australian coverage of prestigious sports events (Lenskyj, 1998). The take home message, therefore, is that female athletes and their achievements are less important than their male counterparts. This is also the case when the sport is a traditionally male sport such as boxing, ski jumping, hammer throwing, triple jump and pole vault where the media representations position the male participants of these sports as the standard against which the women are compared (Pirinen, 1997a; Jones et al, 1999). This serves the purpose of enabling their achievements, in a sport that women have less experience of than men, to be further minimised and negated and to reinforce the view of women's inferior physical ability.

Sportswomen as girls, wives and mothers

The under-representation of sportswomen in the media provides evidence of what has been termed the 'symbolic annihilation' (Tuchman, 1978) of the female athlete (Kane and Greendorfer, 1994). According to Gerbner (1978) 'absence means symbolic annihilation' (p. 44) and, in this way, the media inform us that sportswomen have little value in relation to sportsmen. Moreover, in addition to the amount of media coverage, symbolic annihilation is also evident in the type of coverage when women athletes are featured. Reporters often trivialise and marginalise sportswomen as well as emphasising their appearance and sexuality rather than their sporting performance. Kane and Greendorfer (1994) call this caricaturised femininity which also serves as a form of symbolic annihilation. One recent study of the coverage given to the US gold medal winners at the 1996 Summer Olympics and the 1998 Winter Olympics found that this was more frequent when the sport under discussion was a masculine sport such as soccer and ice-hockey (Jones et al, 1999). To explore caricaturised femininity as a form of symbolic annihilation, two colleagues and I examined the language used in newspaper coverage of female and male athletes participating in the European Athletics Championships, August 1994 (Choi et al, 1996). We got back copies of two British quality newspapers, *The Telegraph* and *The Times*, from 5 to 16 August 1994 and this gave us a total of 21 articles and 16 photographs from *The Telegraph* and 28 articles and 17 photographs from *The Times* for that period. Our thematic analysis revealed two emergent discourses in the texts of the articles on sportswomen that were not evident in the men's: sexuality and personality.

The sexuality discourse emerged in two ways. First from references in the articles to the sportswoman's appearance. This was either in the form of a comment slipped in whilst discussing her athletic performance, for example in an article concerning Marie-Jose Perec's hurdling technique and how much of a challenge she would be to British opponent Sally Gunnell:

> Perec may have the legs, but not yet the perfection.
> (*Times* 12 August 1994)

or in a headline:

> Natural gifts not enough for model runner.
> (*Telegraph* 8 August 1989; referring to the fact that she models)

or as a relatively detailed discussion:

> her considerable beauty – she models and likes to be photographed
> in clinging silver lurex or black feather mini-skirts
> *(Telegraph* 8 August 1994 article on Perec)

> We think of Gunnell as 'nice' because it fits in with her name and
> her unthreatening not-quite-prettiness. (. . . Television does her no
> favours; in the flesh she is far slighter and prettier than on camera,
> and her legs are a knockout.) Gunnell is forever described as having
> girl-next-door appeal.
> *(Telegraph* 13 August 1994)

This form of symbolic annihilation ensures that any emphasis on the sports-woman's performance is diminished by these references to her sexual attractiveness. In a caricaturisation of femininity, she is offered to the reader as sexual object for the masculine gaze. Her sports performance, if acknowledged, is only done within a traditional script of femininity – as secondary to 'man'.

The second way that the sexuality discourse emerged was in the high-lighting of the sportswoman's marital status. Here the emphasis is on the sportswoman as secondary to 'man' as his wife and mother of his children. For example, in an article about Russian sprinter Irina Privalova, reference is made to the fact that she married at 18 and became a mother at 19. Similarly, Phylis Smith is referred to as a 'Midlands mum' with further details of her husband and son later in the article:

> [She] went through the first 300m steadily as her husband and 'slave
> driving' coach Bob had plotted . . . Back home she knew Bob and
> their six-year-old son, Robert, would be going mad.
> *(The Times* 14 August 1994)

What's more Bob is 'the coach who set her on the road to success as a 20-year-old and ended up marrying his protégé' and Smith's £3,000 a year sponsorship is 'totally inadequate to fund her training at the same time as running a family' (ibid). In contrast, there was no discussion of male athletes' wives or children.

The second emergent discourse concerned the sportswomen's personality and like the sexuality discourse, there was no evidence of this in the articles concerning sportsmen. 'Off the track Irina Privalova is warm and amusing' and she has 'a smile almost as broad as her shoulders' *(Times* 10 August 1994). Sally Gunnell is a 'nice' girl who eats chips and this is 'further evidence of her down to earth ordinariness' *(Telegraph* 13 August). And, Phylis Smith is described not only as a Midlands mum, she's an 'ever beaming' one *(Times* 14 August). Later on in the same article:

She remembers how before the Barcelona final, while all her opponents were lined up ashen-faced, she was seen waving and smiling to
the TV cameras . . . Throughout, the smile has never deserted her.

Marie-Jose Perec is not so nice though. She is 'difficult' and 'temperamen-
tal' (*Times* 12 August 1994) and a 'frosty French superstar' (*Times* 14 August
1994) whose 'gold [medal] is unlikely to be accompanied by victory in any
popularity contest' (*Telegraph* 8 August 1994). Other researchers have also
noted references to sportswomen's personalities (e.g. Hilliard, 1984; Kane,
1989; Kane and Greendorfer, 1994) where the focus has been on negative
characteristics such as emotional dependency, anxiety and depression.

Accommodation and resistance

The question begging to be asked is why a sportswoman's sexuality and personality are given more or as much attention as her sporting performance?
Kane and Greendorfer (1994) suggest that it is because the media are both
accommodating the social change that has occurred (increased participation
and greater acceptance of women in sport) and resisting it by reinforcing the
status quo. I would also add that the sportswoman is being used not only to
reinforce sport as masculine but also to reinforce gendered behaviour within
a framework of compulsory heterosexuality. Kolnes (1995) has argued that
the construction of heterosexuality is an organising principle in women's
sports and this will, therefore, influence perceptions of the sportswoman. As
a result of this intricate interaction between the idea of sport as masculine
and the idea of femininity as heterosexual, the sportswoman's appearance,
her sexual desirability (to men) and her status as wife and mother, which are
more congruous with the archetypal feminine stereotype, become the focus.
In other words, Sally Gunnell is an outstanding athlete and a source of
national pride, just like our male athletes are, but she is (hetero)sexually
attractive, she has a boyfriend and wants to have children and is, therefore,
feminine really.

This simultaneous accommodation and resistance results in mixed and
conflicting images being presented that deny sportswomen the power and
prestige that they deserve (Duncan and Hasbrook, 1988). This can also be
seen in visual media portrayals of female athletes. In addition to fewer photographs of sportswomen, the quality of the photograph also differs. In our
study (Choi et al, 1996) we found that the majority of photographs of
sportsmen were active (76%) whilst the majority of sportswomen were passive (58%). Thus, most of the photographs of sportsmen were shots of them
performing in their event (running, jumping, etc.) whilst most of the photographs of sportswomen were taken after the event showing them
stationary and smiling. This renders the physical power of the sportswomen
invisible in the same way that performing gymnastics to music and with a

long ribbon does (Chapter 2, this volume). The viewer is, therefore, provided with only an image of passivity or an image that looks 'nice'. Furthermore, in an analysis of Olympic Games photography appearing in North American magazines, Duncan (1990) found that the photographs of female athletes bore striking resemblance to those of women in soft-core pornography by highlighting their hips, thighs, buttocks, breasts and crotches and by showing female athletes with facial expressions that signify sexual invitation. This fragmentation of 'woman' is consistent with images in art and film where 'woman' is reduced to manageable sexual parts for the masculine gaze (Ussher, 1997). She is seen not as a whole but represented as breasts or legs or face or other body parts.

Duncan (1990) also found that something as subtle as camera angle can emphasise male dominance and female inferiority. She gives an example of two figure skaters, one male and one female, who are being featured in the same article. The photograph of the male places him above the camera and therefore above the viewer suggesting superiority as the person pictured is in an elevated position (the viewer looks up). In contrast, the female figure skater is placed below the camera, below the viewer, suggesting inferiority as she is in a subordinate position (the viewer looks down). Another example that Duncan (1990) gives is that of two swimmers, again both featured in the same article. Their photographs are the same – both show the swimmer's head and upper torso splashing through the water – except for one difference: for the male swimmer the camera is at eye level while for the female swimmer it is above eye level so that the viewer looks down on her.

Glamorous sportswomen are also more likely to be photographed than those who do not fit conventional notions of glamour or beauty. Duncan (1990) noted that in coverage of the 1988 Olympic Games the long hair, stylish clothing and lavish make-up of track and field athlete Florence Griffith Joyner afforded her much more photographic attention than her non-glamorous counterpart Jackie Joyner-Kersee. Both of these athletes had phenomenal successes at the Games but the media clearly favoured 'Flo Jo', who performed in tight clothing cut high above the thigh, wearing make-up, nail polish and jewellery. As a result, her appearance received much more attention than her sporting performance in the news reports (Kane and Greendorfer, 1994). This is particularly interesting given that both these athletes are black and the lack of media interest usually afforded to black athletes. Out of 1,835 front covers of *Sports Illustrated* magazine between 1954 to 1989, only 114 depicted women, of which only 5 were black (Williams and Lumpkin, 1990). The first was of American tennis champion Althea Gibson in 1957. The remaining four were not until the years 1987–1989 and featured Griffith Joyner and Joyner-Kersee. Black women are similarly absent from art and film unless depicted as sexualised, as slave or as 'Black Momma' (Ussher, 1997). Flo Jo, with her sexualised self-presentation, was clearly considered suitable material for the masculine gaze.

Because the vast majority of reporters, editors and directors (in sport and all other media) are men, what is considered newsworthy is based on what they, as men, are familiar with and enjoy. When discussing women, focussing on sexuality provides the male audience with a 'pleasurable "media massage"' (Bate, 1988; p. 207). In the print media, items of interest to women, or about women, are marginalised by being positioned in the Women's Page (Tuchman et al, 1978). Not surprisingly, therefore, it is not just the sportswoman who is under-represented and sexualised by the media, as the absence of women in general or their sexualisation when present is the norm (Bate, 1988). Popular music, for example, has seen a vast increase in the number of female pop stars and all girl groups during the last decade. One of the most notable of these is Madonna whom Fiske (1989) describes as:

an exemplary popular text because she is so full of contradictions – she contains the patriarchal meanings of feminine sexuality and the resisting ones that her sexuality is hers to use as she wishes in ways that do not require masculine approval. Her textuality offers both patriarchy and ways of resisting it in an anxious, unstable tension.

(Fiske, 1989; p. 124; cited in Dibben, 1999)

Thus, as with sportswomen, female pop stars are being accommodated and resisted simultaneously. Also of note, in addition to Madonna, is the all girl group The Spice Girls with whom the revived concept of 'Girl Power' has been associated (Dibben, 1999). However, together with an empowering image of femininity where the Spice Girls present as autonomous, independent, rebellious towards authority and sexually confident, within their music and their videos are presentations of patriarchal constructions of femininity such as voyeuristic display that offers the female body as the object of the masculine gaze (Dibben, 1999). In being positioned in this way, the script of heterosexuality reinforces 'man' as in control and active whilst 'woman', in spite of her resistance, is depicted as passive, as other and marginal to 'man' (Ussher, 1997).

Even when the targetted audience is women, analysis of a recent Olympic Games, Atlanta, 1996, shows the masculine gaze of the producers of American TV coverage to still be operational (Andrews, 1998). That year the US National Broadcasting Company (NBC) decided to target a female audience for these Games as a way of increasing the number of viewers (Andrews, 1998). A greater number of viewers would ensure greater financial success through larger sums of money from advertising. They therefore announced that women's sports would be the focus of their prime time coverage. What did this coverage consist of? According to Andrews (1998) it was what are considered to be feminine appropriate sports such as gymnastics, swimming and diving. Moreover, 'Presumably because they were deemed not to have exuded the appropriate feminine aura, the highly successful US women's basketball, soccer and softball teams, received nothing like the same primetime coverage' (Andrews, 1998; p. 12). Andrews concludes that the NBC coverage, instead of challenging archetypal notions of gender, served to reinforce them.

Women's magazines

It is not just the sports media who communicate the caricaturised femininity of athletes to us. A study of sportswomen in Finnish women's magazines over a 5 year period (Pirinen, 1997b) also found evidence of accommodation and resistance. At one level, the magazine portrayals appeared to be providing an empowering representation for their women readers as features very much promoted the athletes as successful and skilled women. However, closer examination revealed what Pirinen termed a 'disguise of disempowerment' (Pirinen, 1997b; p. 296) by subtly constructing what was acceptable (feminine, heterosexual) and what was not. One way this was seen was in the focus on the athletes' bodies and their attractiveness. Unlike the sports media these representations were not like soft-core pornography (perhaps because they were not intended for a masculine gaze) but two specific representations were distinguishable. These were the feminine-looking body and masculine-looking body. The former body type was clearly privileged through the continual highlighting of the attractiveness of the feminine-looking athlete and by the absence and denigration of the masculine-looking. Pirinen (1997b) provides some examples such as this comment from one magazine writer:

> I came across not a single female athlete with these masculine features, even though I spent hours in the house. Frankly speaking, I have rarely seen so much female beauty at the same time as I did in this house, where the very best of top female athletes had gathered.
> (Pirinen, 1997b; p. 296)

Here the writer informs the reader that masculine features would be unattractive and assures us that sportswomen can still look feminine. Another magazine writer remarked:

> Who are these unforeseen women who go in for powerlifting? Huge, house-sized bundles of muscles casting deadly glances all over? At least Taina Hakala, current record-holder from Seinajoki, does not fit into this image of a massive and aggressive monster. She is a perfectly normal, well-proportioned, shy athlete.
> (Pirinen, 1997b; p. 296)

This writer makes it perfectly clear that the masculine-looking body is unacceptable and, indeed, abnormal. Pirinen (1997b) concludes that for these women's magazines, only the feminine-looking female athlete is acceptable. She also concludes that heterosexual family life is considered the only acceptable lifestyle as detailed descriptions of the athletes' private lives, heterosexual partnerships and children were highlighted. In the case of athletes who were single, references to ex-boyfriends were made: 'She always liked sports and it was her boyfriend at the time who always persuaded her to go down to the gym' (Pirinen, 1997b; p. 298) or descriptions of their ideal husband were given: 'Ritva Jarvinen is a specialist in freestyle swimming. Her future husband – whoever he is – must be an athlete, or at least a sports fan' (Pirinen, 1997b; p. 298). These single women were, therefore, firmly positioned as heterosexual. Such compulsory heterosexuality is also evident in women's magazines in general with advice on how to behave (in and out of bed) in order to get and keep a boyfriend being the main focus (Ussher, 1997).

The threat of the lesbian label

Griffin (1992) has argued that in sport the word femininity is really a code for heterosexuality because of the focus on the physical body which is a symbol of sexuality. Because female athletes are a threat to men's sport and because they behave in a manner that is incongruous with archetypal heterosexual femininity, the lesbian label is very often applied to them in an attempt to ostracise and disempower them (Blinde and Taub, 1992; Griffin, 1992; Krane, 1997a; Veri, 1999). With the increase in women participating in sport after Title IX the lesbian label moved from being applied to all women who participated in sport to only those who did not look feminine (Griffin, 1998). As a result, more feminine-looking athletes are privileged in order that patriarchy can maintain its control of the female athlete through her body and her sexuality. The female athlete is well aware of this and knows that if she does not appear feminine and/or takes part in a sport considered to be unfeminine, she risks the threat of the lesbian label and its consequences (Krane, 1999; Veri, 1999). Some of the negative consequences of not appearing sufficiently feminine include lack of, or adverse, media attention; fewer sponsorship opportunities; negative treatment from coaches, judges, officials and sports administrators; and verbal harassment from sports fans (Kolnes, 1995; Krane, 1999). Any of these alone could potentially ruin a sportswoman's career. To avoid this some sportswomen take care to present themselves as heterosexual in appearance by, for example, wearing feminine clothing, make-up and hairstyles (Kolnes, 1995; Veri, 1999), and in behaviour such as being seen with and talking about their boyfriends at great length and in avoiding known or suspected lesbians for fear of being suspected of being lesbian themselves (Lenskyj, 1997).

According to Kolnes it was important for the sportswomen in her study to be accepted both as women and as athletes and that 'for some women a sporting career is indivisible from a sexual career' (Kolnes, 1995; p. 68). To accommodate this they need to balance feminine characteristics with mas-culine ones, hence the emphasis on heterosexual feminine appearance. For example, one soccer player reports that she has long hair because she is a soccer player, that short hair looks boyish and by having long hair she can 'compensate for playing in shorts, gear and socks' (Kolnes, 1995; p. 66). But, as one participant, Sue, in a study by Young (1997) remarked: 'They want you to be a girl, I want to be a girl, but I want you to watch my sport and like me when I do it. The truth is, I don't know if rugby can be played in any "feminine" way' (p. 301).

Often the enhancement of femininity is a requirement imposed upon the athletes by coaches or administrators. For example, the Ladies Professional Golf Association (LPGA) have employed an image consultant to help the golfers with hairstyles, make-up, etc. in order to portray a suitably feminine image (Festle, 1996). They have also promoted those golfers who are mar-ried and have children more than those who are not and published a calendar of golfers posing in swimsuits alongside publicly denying the exis-tence of any lesbians on the tour (Burton-Nelson, 1991). Festle (1996) notes that media coverage, corporate sponsorship, prize money, and revenue from the LPGA tour have since increased significantly. Another example is the 1996 Olympic softball team who appeared on the Oprah Winfrey Show. For this TV appearance, which Griffin refers to as a 'heterosexual drag show' (Griffin, 1998; p. 71), the athletes had to have a makeover and wear dresses and high heels. Other coaches have instructed their athletes to dress in a feminine way, to wear make-up and to 'not look butch' (Krane, 1997b; p. 151).

Emphasising heterosexual femininity can also be required of athletes through the clothing that they must wear for the performance of their sport. The 1990 Canadian hockey team had to wear pink uniforms because of the perception of women's hockey as masculine and because of accusations of lesbianism (Krane, 1999). Whilst some of the players resented this, they complied in order to protect the image of the team. In some track and field events and aesthetic sports such as gymnastics and diving, recent years have seen a trend towards tight and revealing sportswear that highlights the sex-ualised body. Says Liz McColgan, British long distance runner, in an interview for *Cosmopolitan* magazine: 'When I began running, we just had a simple leotard which cut across the thigh. Now women are expected to run in high-cut bikini strips. Everything has to be on show and everything has to look gorgeous' (Harper, 1997; p. 64). In Kolnes' (1995) study some athletes felt that this objectification was acceptable in order to promote women's sport but for others it was not as they felt uncomfortable with so much of their body being visible:

I had to run with such gear once [high-cut bikini strips] . . . and then decided that I would never do it again because I felt extremely uncomfortable wearing it. And I know there are other women at a high international level who have the same opinion. To me it is most important to run from A to B, and not that people stare at me along the track.

(Kolnes, 1995; p. 68)

For some athletes from non-Western cultures, the dilemmas are enormous as the requirement to have everything on show means they cannot participate in international level competition. Muslim women, for example, can participate in sports but they must cover their bodies with a *hajib* (a head to toe black robe plus veil). Muslim nations, therefore, do not allow their female athletes to compete in the Olympic Games, as this would mean their being seen in public with exposed flesh. When the Algerian athlete Hassiba Boulmerka defiantly competed in the 1992 Barcelona games 1500 metres wearing running shorts and vest, her country did not celebrate her gold medal on her return (Prince, 1998). Instead, she was strongly criticised by the national mosque and, according to Prince (1998), has moved to another country due to the harassment that followed.

Lesbian athletes

The fear of the lesbian label creates a very heterosexist and homonegative[3] environment within women's sports which can create disharmony amongst the sportswomen, thereby weakening the threat to patriarchy. It is also doubly damaging for lesbian athletes. That is, not only do they have to deal with society's negative perception of female athletes as lesbian, they also have to contend with anti-lesbianism within the sports environment that can come from all its members (Krane, 1997b). In 1991, the coach of the US Penn State women's basketball team, Rene Portland, publicly announced that she did not allow lesbians on her teams. Krane's study of university athletes revealed that coaches and administrators removed lesbians from the teams or threatened to remove them or call their parents if they did not behave in 'an appropriate manner' (Krane, 1997b; p. 151). One participant reported that during her first visit to a university where she was being considered, the athletic director explicitly told her that if she was a lesbian, this would not be acceptable:

Another thing you need to think about when you come to school is the fact that there will be lesbian athletes in a lot of athletic programs. So, you need to consider this because we are moving towards straightening our programs out, and if you have an interest like this you need to reconsider or you need to fall in line.

(Krane, 1997b; p. 152)

Krane's study further revealed that along with the coaches, the team members also invoked the lesbian label. One way in which this occurred was in commenting on who was gay on their team or others. Often this may not have been true such as 'Oh, the softball and basketball teams – they're all lesbians' (Krane, 1997b; p. 153). Other ways of invoking the label were through derogatory name calling, commenting, gossiping and telling jokes about gay people and making fun of known lesbians on the team. Although often hurt by this, none of the women challenged the negative attitudes for fear of drawing attention to themselves and revealing their sexual identity.

Given the small number of known lesbians in sport it can be concluded that most lesbian athletes and coaches choose to remain silent about their sexual identity because of the potential risks such as ostracism, loss of sponsorship and employment. Consider, for example, tennis player Billie Jean King who was publicly outed in 1981 when her former girlfriend sued her for palimony. King subsequently lost most of her commercial sponsors and received no public support from the tennis world (Griffin, 1998). Rumour has it that one major sponsor of the US Women's Tennis Association tour threatened to withdraw its sponsorship if anyone spoke of homosexuality on the tour (Griffin, 1998). Burton-Nelson (1991) notes that known lesbian tennis player Martina Navratilova had far less sponsorship than would be expected of a player of her calibre and far less than Chris Evert whose heterosexual femininity had been heavily promoted. More recently, however, lesbian athletes such as professional golfer Muffin Spencer-Devlin and professional mountain biker Missy Giove have been open about their sexual identity without any apparent negative repercussions. They continue to attract high levels of sponsorship and therefore provide new images of women in sport.

Performing femininity

Of her research participants Kolnes asserts that:

> One of the worse things that can happen to these women is to be taken for being a man or for being a lesbian. They want to be recognised as women and to look 'proper' (that is feminine) even though they are soccer players. What we see is that female athletes who are acting in areas which traditionally are connected with masculinity, are submitting themselves in a way which makes it possible to prove to themselves and to others that they actually are women.
>
> (Kolnes, 1995; p. 67)

Kolnes (1995) has termed this 'gender performance', which is similar to Butler's (1990) concept of 'performing femininity' and Ussher's (1997) 'negotiating femininity'. Butler (1990) contends that performing femininity is not necessarily an active choice. She argues that we perform gender through social learning and this serves to perpetuate gender appropriate behaviour which in turn reinforces cultural norms. That is, because women are socialised to behave in feminine appropriate ways, this occurs without challenge and such behaviours then become fixed and considered to be natural. However, Ussher (1997) asserts that women are not passive dupes who simply accept the scripts of femininity. She argues that they actively negotiate these scripts and reconcile the contradictions. From Kolnes' (1995) study and the various other examples above, it should be clear that sportswomen are actively engaged in this very complex process. The athlete knows that her sporting career may be assisted if she performs heterosexual femininity and, as exemplified by the soccer player above, she may actively and consciously choose to do so to a greater or lesser degree and in many different ways. Similarly, lesbian athletes are another example of sportswomen who consciously and actively choose to perform heterosexual femininity.

Ussher (1997) has proposed that there are at least four 'performances' or positions that women can take up in their negotiations of femininity: 'doing girl', 'being girl', 'resisting girl' and 'subverting girl' with '"girl" being that archetypal fantasy of perfect femininity we see framed within the boundaries of heterosexual sexuality and romance' (Ussher, 1997; p. 445). Thus, 'being girl' is described as the role of being the archetypal feminine woman who believes in the differences between women and men as natural. This position is probably not common amongst sportswomen as sport is a traditionally masculine domain. In contrast, the position of 'doing girl' is where the woman chooses to follow the script of archetypal femininity when it is considered to be, and only for as long as it is, to her advantage. This position is probably very common amongst sportswomen and is, perhaps, synonymous with Kolnes' (1995) gender performance where feminine appearance and behaviour are emphasised to assist the sportswoman's career. 'Resisting girl' is when the woman chooses to resist or ignore the archetypal script and many, if not all, sportswomen could be considered to fulfil this position simply because they are sportswomen but in particular women who participate in masculine sports such as boxing and lesbian athletes. The fourth position of 'subverting girl' is when women subvert femininity and publicly and openly parody traditional scripts of gender. An example of this position might be the female competitive bodybuilder who presents her muscular body on stage but with feminine adornments and posing routines (see Chapter 4, this volume).

It is important to note that there may be many more positions that a woman can adopt and that the positions are not fixed; they are fluid with the woman moving between them depending on the situation and context. The positions are also plural in that women can take up more than one at a time. For example, probably the best-known example of an athlete 'doing girl' was the sprinter Flo Jo, mentioned earlier in this chapter. During the 1988 Olympics she consciously emphasised her heterosexual feminine appearance whilst performing her sport. Another is the high jumper Amy Acuff, mentioned in Chapter 1. Both of these could be described as both doing and resisting girl simultaneously. In another way, so could lesbian athletes as they obviously 'resist girl' by choosing a lesbian identity but in the sports context when they hide their sexual orientation and emphasise heterosexual femininity they are 'doing girl'.

For other athletes 'doing girl' is more of an issue when they are not participating in their sport. For example, Krane et al (1998) found that female university athletes were concerned about their muscular bodies and whether they looked masculine only in social settings (see Chapter 5, this volume). In the sporting environment their bodies were appropriate for the performance of their sport, but outside of this setting it was another matter, leading to 'doing girl' off court and 'resisting girl' on court.

It should now be apparent that sportswomen are not simply victims of the process of gendering. Gender is a performance that they (and all women) take part in but it is also a performance that is influenced by the woman's sociocultural context and the representations of femininity that are available at the time. Sometimes this does not give the woman complete freedom to choose the position(s) she would most prefer. In the case of sport, the sociocultural context is one where the sportswoman's femininity is questioned and where her sport is considered less important than men's sport. It is one where images of her are sexualised for the masculine gaze in both accommodating and resisting her. Sportswomen are now equalling and surpassing records previously set by men. Indeed, Kane has pointed out that there now exists 'a sport *continuum* in which many women routinely outperform many men, and in some cases, women outperform most – if not all – men in a variety of sports and physical skills/activities. The acknowledgement of such a continuum could provide a direct assault on traditional beliefs about sport – and gender itself' (Kane, 1995; p. 193). Instead of acknowledging this continuum, by focussing on her sexuality, by trivialising and objectifying her, the sportswoman is made subordinate and therefore less fearful. And let us not forget that sport is a multi-billion pound/dollar industry where sponsorship and ticket sales depend on an acceptable public image. Unfortunately, this acceptability masks the positive message that we could take home (i.e. her athletic abilities are equal to men's) and instead tells us that she is 'other' and that she is not and cannot be equal to men.

Notes

1 These figures were sent to me on an information sheet available to WSF members.
2 Information on this study was provided by Dr Attila Szabo, Senior Lecturer at Nottingham Trent University and supervisor of this research.
3 Following Krane (1997b) this term is used to refer to prejudice and discrimination against non-heterosexuals as opposed to the term homophobia which means an irrational fear or intolerance of homosexuality.

4

THE MUSCULAR WOMAN

In the previous chapter it was illustrated how femininity and feminine appearances can be important to, and have implications for, female athletes. This chapter will explore this further by examining the female bodybuilder because it could be argued that she poses the greatest conflict of all to the masculine domain of sport. Bodybuilding is an activity that builds muscles and the aim, according to Daniels (1992), is to develop 'traditional masculine he-man dimension' (p. 371). Thus, lifting weights and bodybuilding are truly masculine domains – indeed, weightlifting only became an Olympic sport for women for the first time in the Sydney 2000 Games. Within the world of bodybuilding as well as amongst scholars, considerable debates and controversies surrounding the female bodybuilder have ensued and these could be said to epitomise wider controversies surrounding femininity and what it means to be a (physically active) woman. More so than most other sportswomen, female bodybuilders challenge society's gender boundaries (Daniels, 1992). Female bodybuilders have muscles as big as, if not bigger than, their male counterparts. They are physically very strong and can lift heavier weights than many men, and many male bodybuilders. These attributes are not congruent with archetypal femininity.

The sport of bodybuilding

Bodybuilding is a unique sport in that whilst lifting weights is the activity during training, the aims of training and of competition are different. For the weightlifter or powerlifter,[1] the aim is to lift the maximum amount of weight, but for the bodybuilder, in competition the appearance of the whole body is what is judged and not the strength or the efficiency of the muscles. The training requirement of the bodybuilder, therefore, is to achieve muscular hypertrophy in order to meet specific criteria of muscular size, shape and definition. Whilst the weightlifter and powerlifter does, of course, achieve muscular enhancement, this is a by-product of the sport and not the primary intention as it is with the bodybuilder. In competition, the requirement for the bodybuilder is to pose on stage in front of a panel of judges, flexing his or her muscles to show their size and shape.[2] The weight training is a means to an end as this is what causes the muscles to grow and develop. Outside of the competition season, known as the 'off season', bodybuilders train with heavy weights and aim to increase muscle size. Then, when preparing for a competition they train with lighter weights in order to shape the muscle that has been built. Most crucial (and most difficult) of all for competition preparation is dieting – the high protein and low carbohydrate combination and the decreasing total number of calories as the competition date approaches. This is essential to reduce body fat to very low levels (without losing muscle as well) in order for muscle size and definition to be visible (known as being 'ripped'). This aesthetically 'perfect' body, during competition, is judged subjectively by a panel of mostly, if not totally, men in both women's and men's competitions.

The female bodybuilding competition

Defining the aesthetically 'perfect' body (in bodybuilding terms) is fairly straightforward for male bodybuilders but far from straightforward for women. For the male bodybuilders, the judges make their decisions strictly on muscular size and symmetry. The bigger he is, the more likely he is to win. The female bodybuilder, however, can be judged to be too big and not feminine enough. The 1984 semi-documentary film *Pumping Iron II: The Women* illustrated this very well. This cult film tells the story of a women's bodybuilding competition with real life bodybuilding champions and International Federation of Bodybuilders (IFBB) personnel playing themselves with the masculinity–femininity debate at the centre of the film's plot. In the film the extremely muscular Bev Francis is considered too masculine to win, whilst the less muscular but very pretty and very feminine Rachel McLish is considered the favourite to win. In the end, neither wins; another real life elite bodybuilder, Carla Dunlap, who is positioned midway along the Francis–McLish continuum, does.

In one scene the judges of the competition confer on what the word 'femininity' means in this context and Joe Weider, Chairman of the IFBB, describes the female bodybuilder thus:

> What we are looking for is something that's right down the middle. A woman who has a certain amount of aesthetic femininity, but yet has that muscle tone to show that she is an athlete.
>
> (cited in Holmlund, 1989; p. 41)

Thus, different competitive categories and rules exist for the women that are not in place for the men and the IFBB rules for the 1999 Ms Olympia state that:

> First and foremost the judge must bear in mind that this is a woman's bodybuilding competition and that the goal is to find an

ideal female physique. Therefore, the most important aspect is shape – a muscular yet feminine shape. The other aspects are similar to those described for the male physique but muscular development must not be carried to such an excess that it resembles the massive musculature of the male physique.

(http://www.ifbb.com/amarules/app1.html)

There are no references to a masculine shape in the men's competition rules. There are also no references to excessive musculature. The female bodybuilder, therefore, is required to limit her sporting achievement for fear of becoming, or appearing, unfeminine. This is analogous to telling women runners that they can only run so fast, or high jumpers that they can only jump so high before they jeopardise their femininity. The focus is not just on the female athlete's sports performance (in this case her musculature and symmetry); her feminine appearance is equally, or possibly more important.

What this ideal female physique and feminine shape might be is totally subjective. One official interviewed by Lowe (1998) seemed to think that it means not having any muscles at all:

Some of the [female] bodybuilders, if you look at them, look like men. When they flex a bicep, it's a real bicep.

(Lowe, 1998; p. 156)

Thus, he seems to believe that only men should have real muscles, which seems a rather strange view given that we are all born with the same kind of muscles. Women do not have fake ones. Other judges, such as Tracy, below, have different views, however:

Well, of course, female bodybuilders have got to have muscle and I look at the shape of the muscle in each muscle group. And the one with the best overall shape, muscular shape, really is who I go for. If she's big, and she's got really good shape, and she still looks feminine, and I've got somebody else who is not so big and has equal shape, I will go for the bigger one as long as she looks feminine.

(Lowe, 1998; p. 114)

This still does not tell us what is 'feminine' although according to the IFBB 1999 rules it includes the way the woman walks:

Competitors shall also be assessed on whether or not they carry themselves in a graceful manner while walking to and from their position on stage.

(http://www.ifbb.com/amarules/app1.html)

Asked by Lowe how she judges femininity, Tracy replied:

> Well, you can tell her hips from her waist. In other words, that she has a waistline. No facial hair, makeup is on, her hair is in a flattering style. The way she carries herself on stage, her posing routine.
>
> (Lowe, 1998; p. 114)

Again, these criteria are totally subjective. How does one measure how flattering a competitor's hairstyle is? Other sports such as gymnastics and figure skating also have an element of subjective assessment but unlike bodybuilding, these sports have objective criteria to aid the judging process. For example, a triple backward somersault is more difficult to execute than a single forward one so the successful execution of the former will undoubtedly earn more marks than the latter. There are no such markers in the bodybuilding competition. This can be problematic in both the men's and the women's competitions, but in the women's there is the additional factor of the judge's subjective assessment of feminine appearance. Whether the male bodybuilder looks masculine is never an issue in the judging of the men's competition. The differing views of femininity lead to inconsistencies and contradictions amongst the judges such as a competitor being placed first by half of the judges but last by the other half (Mansfield and McGinn, 1993; Lowe, 1998).

The female bodybuilder, therefore, needs to emphasise her appearance of femininity and detract from her muscularity and hope she gets it right for those judges residing on the day. She does this by wearing ribbons in her hair, make-up and nail polish and many also have cosmetic surgery such as silicone breast implants and take anabolic steroids to enhance muscular definition (Hargreaves, 1994; Guthrie et al, 1994). Donna Hartley, a former British champion, explains what is required in an article in *Bodybuilding Monthly* magazine:

> Also little things about going on stage are vital. Some people don't bother to tan properly, they don't do their hair or nails. It's important that all these things are done as they all add up to the end package. I also think if women bodybuilders have cropped short hair and they are muscular they look mannish.
>
> (cited in Mansfield and McGinn, 1993; p. 63)

Daniels (1992) has proposed that femininity is central to judging as according to his ethnographic research, most winners are blond with 'large hairdo's'; they are often dressed in pink bikinis, or other pastel colours, and wear heavy make-up. This has also been remarked upon by women bodybuilders themselves (Guthrie et al, 1994). Moreover, as someone who has viewed many bodybuilding competitions (and taken part in a small number),

I would also argue that a more feminine posing routine, such as one that contains graceful and dance like movements, can contribute to competition success.

Bev Francis, former world champion bodybuilder, is a good example of the 'emphasising femininity to win' phenomenon. Former Australian record holder in the shot-put and six times World Powerlifting Champion, Francis took up bodybuilding in 1983 (whilst continuing with powerlifting). Because of her years of powerlifting her musculature was exceptionally large and she consistently failed to win bodybuilding competitions on the grounds that her body resembled that of a male physique. She therefore gave up powerlifting, reduced her musculature, dyed her hair blond and won the IFBB Women's World Professional Bodybuilding Championship in 1987. However, the Ms Olympia title (the most prestigious and most coveted of all the professional bodybuilding competitions) continued to elude her despite further reductions and reshaping to her musculature over a period of years to adopt a more aesthetic and feminine shape, and by perming her hair and having facial cosmetic surgery. After she placed second in the Ms Olympia in 1990 and again in 1991, she retired from professional bodybuilding. It cannot have been easy for her to change her body from what it was but change it she did. How dramatic these changes were can only be appreciated from pictures of her in bodybuilding magazines over the years. Without doubt, from these pictures one can see her become more 'feminine' with blonder, curlier hair, more make-up, pink outfits and more feminine poses. (For pictures, see http://www.bevfrancis.com/francisfactor.htm)

In contrast to Bev Francis, Cory Everson managed to get it 'right', as is evidenced by her winning the Ms Olympia title six times in a row. Although now retired from professional bodybuilding and pursuing a career in Hollywood, she is still featured in bodybuilding magazines as the model female bodybuilder (Ndalianis, 1995). Small, blonde, glamorous, full breasted and muscular, she managed to find the winning formula of balance between her muscular and feminine emphasis through surgical breast enhancement, feminine posing routines that are dance-like and graceful, as well as suitable hairstyles and make-up which Mansfield and McGinn (1993) suggest are 'reminiscent of the style adopted by the fictional women of Dallas' (p. 63).

This situation is very frustrating for those who believe that female bodybuilders should be able to achieve as much muscularity as they can and thus be judged as male bodybuilders are. One national level competitor interviewed by Lowe (1998) explained how she felt when told that female bodybuilders can be too muscular:

> What kind of fucking garbage is that?! Come on, this is *bodybuilding*, this is about muscles, this is about displaying the best you've got! We're being told to tone it down . . . Every other sport in the

world, you do the best you can do, and now women are being told to tone it down and I think it's such a hard thing to do.

(Lowe, 1998; p. 91)

According to Lowe it was over the period of the 1991 and 1992 competition seasons that the excessive musculature debate reached a turning point within the world of bodybuilding, resulting in greater efforts to pull the women back. In 1991 the Ms Olympia was televised live on ESPN (an American 24 hour sports channel) for the first time but was allegedly not well received by the viewers (Lowe, 1998). Letters and telephone calls were received by both ESPN and the IFBB from viewers expressing horror at a sport where the women look like men. As a result, the bodybuilding federations began to limit the women's muscular development in earnest. This was apparent in subsequent professional competitions where the most muscular women did not win and where judging inconsistencies between competitions became very obvious (Lowe, 1998). At one international professional competition in 1992 the winner was 'one of the least muscular and most "traditionally" attractive female bodybuilders' (Lowe, 1998; p. 111). One bodybuilding judge interviewed by Lowe (1998) within a year of this competition when 'the sport was still reeling from the fallout over that show's decision' (Lowe, 1998; pp. 111–112) explained that just as clothing comes in and out of fashion over time, so too do large muscles in female bodybuilders. However, as Lowe (1998) points out, the trend in men's bodybuilding has been and continues to be towards larger muscles and does not wax and wane between larger and smaller. This difference could not be explained by the judge.

Another way of limiting the women competitors was the announcement that drug testing for anabolic steroid use would take place at the 1992 Ms Olympia (there was no such announcement for the Mr Olympia). These drugs, which are synthetic derivatives of the hormone testosterone, are widely used by bodybuilders (and many other athletes[3]) as they promote muscle growth and improve sports performance but they can also have deleterious physical and psychological health effects (Choi et al, 1989; Choi, 1993; Yesalis, 1993). They are, therefore, on the International Olympic Committee's (IOC) list of banned substances. In line with IOC policy, the IFBB requires competitors to be tested but leaves the responsibility for this solely with the competition promoters who do not always enforce this for a couple of reasons. Firstly, the cost of the test is very high and testing would therefore reduce profits. Secondly, testing reduces the number of bodybuilders who would compete, especially those who are larger and more famous with greater capacity to pull in the crowds. This also reduces profits. Conversely, competition promoters do not want hugely muscular women taking part as it is the more feminine who are considered more attractive and appealing to the fans. As a result, although anabolic steroid use is far more prevalent amongst male bodybuilders than it is amongst female body-builders, the latter have always been subjected to drug testing more often than their male counterparts (Lowe, 1998). The reasons put forward for this are undoubtedly related to the issue of feminine appearance and how much muscle should the female bodybuilder have before she crosses the boundary into a masculine appearance. Although couched as concerns for the women's health because, so the argument goes, testosterone is present in higher dosages in men and therefore more natural and less dangerous, anabolic steroid use is as dangerous to the health of both sexes. Moreover, it is the male bodybuilders, not females, who are getting ill and dying from the abuse of a variety of performance enhancing drugs because the problem is greater amongst them (Lowe, 1998). Nonetheless, the assumption that muscularity and femininity are incongruous has kept the restriction of anabolic steroid use on women in order to restrict their muscular growth. As one official interviewed by Lowe about the drug testing of female bodybuilders stated: 'It's okay for a man to be big and masculine and freaky. For a female, you start looking like a drag queen' (Lowe, 1998; p. 80). The primary concern, therefore, is not the women's health but in maintaining the gender order of society.

Resistance or compliance

In popular media it has sometimes been proposed that female bodybuilding is the ultimate expression of feminism. For example, an editorial in *Muscle and Fitness* magazine claimed that women's bodybuilding 'has given woman the opportunity to claim her equality' and 'is one of the strongest expressions to come out of the feminist movement' (Weider, 1990). In addition, feminist scholars have argued that women's very participation in bodybuilding rep-resents a resistance to the dominant discourse of femininity (e.g. Bartky, 1988; Heywood, 1998) and because of this Heywood (1998) in her cultural study of female bodybuilding has likened it to a form of political activism on a par with feminism. Female bodybuilders insist that it is they who are solely responsible for the way they look and that they are empowered by the con-trol they have over their bodies which have been developed according to their standards (not society's) and which is reflected in other aspects of their lives (Duff and Hong, 1984; Miller and Penz, 1991; Guthrie and Castelnuovo, 1992). For example, champion bodybuilder Sue Price says: 'I'm feminine but I'm strong; I'm a woman but I'm not weak' (Heywood, 1998; p. 34). And from Skye Ryland: 'Thanks to bodybuilding . . . I feel more alive and sexy than ever before' (Heywood, 1998; p. 34).

But in many respects it is not the case that female bodybuilders reject the traditional notion of woman as desirable sex object. As described above, the constraints placed upon the competitive female bodybuilder mandate com-pliance with the discourse of archetypal femininity. Female bodybuilding, therefore, is contradictory, involving both compliance and resistance (Bolin, 1992; Hall, 1996). Guthrie and Castelnuovo (1992) also concede that female bodybuilding can represent both resistance and compliance but suggest that this might depend on whether the woman takes part in competitions or not. As the competitive female bodybuilder is well aware of femininity as the critical component for winning she attempts to shape her body, and her on-stage behaviour, accordingly. Bev Francis, described above, is a good example of this, as are the unhealthy practices of cosmetic surgery to enlarge breasts and anabolic steroid abuse to enhance muscular definition which have also been reported as common ways of appearing more feminine (Guthrie et al, 1994). Thus, as with other female athletes (see Chapter 3, this volume), the competitive bodybuilder takes part in what Kolnes (1995) has termed gender performance, or as Ussher (1997) has described, she 'does girl', or maybe even 'subverts girl'.

The non-competitive female bodybuilder, on the other hand, according to Guthrie and Castelnuovo (1992) does not have to concern herself with gender performance – in theory. She can supposedly build as much muscle as she desires, rejecting the standard definitions of femininity, constructing her own definition of the ideal body – she is, therefore, resisting. However, there is still pressure to comply from family and friends. Competitive bodybuilder or not, for many bodybuilding women, resisting narrow definitions of femininity were their primary motives for taking up bodybuilding but they also believed that some measure of compliance was necessary for them to actively engage in transforming how women are perceived by society (Guthrie and Castelnuovo, 1992; Bredemeier et al, 1991). This is not an easy process, however:

> This was the message you get, 'If you're going to have muscles, you damn well better be feminine' . . . I didn't want to be a man . . . I kind of felt sort of caught in the twilight zone.
>
> (from Bredemeier et al, 1991; p. 101)

According to Miller and Penz (1991) female bodybuilders reject conventional standards of femininity 'in conformity with the traditional feminine norm' (p. 152). Jane, who had been competing successfully for 3 years at time of interview (Choi, 1999b), describes how and why she 'does girl' in order to resist. She accepts that people do not find large muscular women attractive and in order to change people's perceptions she feels the right image has to be presented.

> I can see both arguments really. It's not seen as being feminine to be largely muscled . . . it's publicity as well because you've got to market yourself and if you are on stage and you are big and muscly, it's not going to be as attractive to people . . . I'm looking

> to promote the [body] building in a positive way with a healthier image. I'd rather people still look at me and think that I have a more feminine look.
>
> (Choi, 1999b)

This is not just on stage while competing but also in everyday life such as in the way she dresses:

> I've got an image to portray and if I'm going walking around in like a short skirt and stuff, people are just going to think that I'm a man dressed up . . . I'm better wearing a long flowing dress and covering myself up and try and make myself look a bit more elegant.
>
> (Choi, 1999b)

and in the way she behaves:

> I think you work harder at trying to get people to understand that just because you've got muscles doesn't mean to say that you're actually masculine or that you think differently to another woman. That really gets up my nose when people look at you and they think that you are going to be masculine.
>
> (Choi, 1999b)

Similar views about presenting an image of the feminine bodybuilder have been expressed by Bev Francis in her manual of bodybuilding (Francis, 1989), who also emphasises wearing loose clothing which hides muscular development. Whilst Francis does not explicitly discuss fulfilling femininity requirements, according to Obel (1996), this is what she is concerned with. Rather than resisting traditional femininity, Francis is emphasising it in order to enhance the acceptability of women's bodybuilding and bodybuilding in general (Obel, 1996). And, let us not forget that as with other sports, bodybuilding is a money-making industry so an acceptable image of femininity means improved chances of recognition, sponsorship and access to resources. Like the elite female athlete, the elite female bodybuilder's career depends on her 'doing girl' (see Chapter 3, this volume).

In the January 1993 edition of *Flex* magazine, which is described by Ndalianis (1995) as depicting the catch-22 situation of the female bodybuilder, the responses of a number of elite female bodybuilders to the possibility of their wearing g-strings and high heels in competition were published. Much opposition was expressed because of sexual associations, with the women stating that this was a sport that they have dedicated their lives to and 'We're up there to compete, not entertain men's fantasies' (Ndalianis, 1995; p. 20). However, as Ndalianis points out, this text with its strong message of resistance, is accompanied by images of these bodybuilders in erotic poses, wearing g-strings and high heels – a strong message of compliance. Ndalianis (1995) points out how little control the women have over these images which are mandated as part of their publicity contract and without this contract, they have no career in this sport. The resisting woman, therefore, is being 'tamed' through forced compliance with the norms of heterosexual femininity (Schulze, 1990).

Flex appeal

As with the elite female athletes in Chapters 2 and 3, the balance between compliance and resistance, or doing and resisting girl, is a delicate one and always sure to be controversial as it presents dilemmas for the athletes and for society. In the late 1980s a new American bi-monthly bodybuilding magazine for women appeared on the shelves with the aim of promoting women's bodybuilding. In addition to articles on training, diet and nutrition, fashion and beauty, it contained the coverage of women's competitions and women bodybuilders that are lacking in other bodybuilding magazines. As with sports media coverage in general (see Chapter 3, this volume), bodybuilding coverage is primarily male bodybuilding. Although there has been a growth in images of female bodybuilders in these magazines during the 1990s, they are less often featured in their own right. The feature is usually about a male bodybuilder with photographs of him posing with his bodybuilding girlfriend.

This new magazine, therefore, was very welcome. It claimed to be promoting a positive image of female bodybuilders by depicting them as beautiful as well as strong. However, beauty appeared to mean sexually desirable to men as one criticism of some of the visual representations of the female bodybuilders in this new magazine was that they were merely providing pin up material for men. However, others agreed that this was the image they wanted to see portrayed:

> I'm an outspoken, opinionated feminist and in my opinion your photos are SUPERB . . . I'd like to live to see the day *Playboy* comes out with a centrefold like one of yours.
> (from Letters to the Editor, *Female Bodybuilding*, September 1989)

Indeed, *Playboy* has referred to *Female Bodybuilding* as 'a grabber of a publication' (Ndalianis, 1995). *Flex*, an American monthly published by the IFBB guru Joe Weider, has recently been running a series of photographic features on women bodybuilders. The photographs are of the women in their off season condition when they are carrying more body fat and not looking as muscular as they do in competition. This is the more usual state for the woman bodybuilder as she spends the majority of her time *not* in competition. This condition has been found to be considered more attractive. In a study of 60 male and female English undergraduates who viewed photographs of a female bodybuilder with her face blanked out, the bodybuilder in the non-competition state was rated significantly more positively on a range of adjectives than the bodybuilder in the competitive state (Pugh, 1993). *Flex* describes this as 'a much more naturally attractive condition' (why is less muscle more attractive?) and in her competition condition she 'can be perceived as threatening' (to whom and how?). So:

> To exhibit this real, natural side of women bodybuilders, Flex has been presenting pictorials of female competitors in softer condition. We hope this approach dispels the myth of female-bodybuilder masculinity and proves what role models they truly are.
>
> (*Flex*, June 1996, August 1997)

How is this real, natural and attractive condition illustrated? With photography akin to soft porn – the women pouting, posing naked or semi-naked in sexual positions such as rear view shots of them bending over or frontal shots of them sitting with legs spread apart. They are not, therefore, role models as sportswomen but as sex objects. Thus, the more natural and attractive woman is the less muscular, soft, vulnerable and (hetero) sexually available woman. Under the guise of promoting woman the bodybuilder, woman the sex object, available for the masculine gaze, is promoted instead. This does not occur with the male bodybuilder as he is represented as a bodybuilder, not a sexual being. Thus, his sporting achievements are celebrated but hers are diminished or rendered invisible. As Heywood has pointed out, this reinforces traditional views that the female athlete is inferior to the male athlete and no matter how good she may be, she is still a woman 'subject to all the traditional ideas about women and diminution' (Heywood, 1998; p. 98).

Sex appeal

The bodybuilding woman must be feminine – she must have muscular development, but not too much, and she must still be sexy. These are the rules for the women who wish to play the masculine game of bodybuilding where flex appeal is what the judges look for. However, in addition to different competition rules for the women, there are also two different categories of women's bodybuilding. The first is the Physique class, which is what I have described above. The other category is the Figure/fitness class (there is no equivalent for the men), which has really grown in popularity during the 1990s and is like a 'fitness' version of the beauty contest (for comparison see Figures 4.1 and 4.2).

Figure 4.1 Ms Physique. (Courtesy of John Plummer.)

The physical appearance of the [figure/fitness] competitors must portray a softer appearance to those of the female Physique categories and their aesthetic and symmetrical qualities are of paramount importance compared to their muscularity. However, they must display a physique that has been well trained while being penalised if their condition is too muscular.

Judging guidelines of The Association of Natural Bodybuilders, (personal communication, November 1997)

Thus, in the Physique category muscular development and femininity are allegedly of equal importance but in the Figure/fitness category their feminine shape, their grace and their sexuality comes first whilst muscularity, which must be much less than the Physique woman, takes second place. The difference between the two competition categories was explained to me by Sandra:

Figure/fitness class is somebody who actually looks like a woman and the Physique class is somebody who doesn't care, who needs to try and pack as much muscle on that body as any of the male competitors.

Figure 4.2 Ms Figure. (Courtesy of John Plummer.)

Helen, a gym instructor, who at time of interview (Spring 1997) was hoping to compete in Figure/fitness competition explained:

> [Physique women] don't have to be perfect. They don't go on beauty whatsoever. Fitness is definitely harder. If you haven't got the looks or, you won't get anywhere in fitness. It's more of a beauty competition as well.

Figure/fitness competitors therefore aim to emphasise not their flex appeal but their sex appeal. Under some rules they are allowed to wear high heels on stage as opposed to having to appear barefoot like the men and the Physique women. They may wear g-strings (thong bikinis), which are considered indecent in the men's and Physique women's categories. Their poses are also more 'feminine'. For example, to display the size of the bicep muscle, typically one holds the arm out sideways at shoulder height, bends the elbow so that the forearm is at right angles to the upper arm and clenches the fist hard in order to tense the bicep. Under some rules, Figure/fitness women must perform this pose without clenching the fist, the hand and fingers in a graceful position. They also usually stand in positions that look sexual and I have on occasions seen them on the floor posing on all fours looking sexually inviting. As a result of this emphasis on sexuality, male members of the audience make lewd remarks, wolf whistle and behave as if they are at an erotic show. This is not generally how they behave whilst watching Physique women. During these competitions they behave as they do whilst watching male bodybuilders.

It is for this reason that Sandra, above, has chosen not to compete. She is not a Physique bodybuilder because she would not like to have very developed muscles because, to her, 'it's unnatural for a woman to look like that'. Nevertheless, if she were to compete she would not choose to do so in the Figure/fitness category.

> I would prefer to compete in a Physique class. Not because I like the muscles but because men look at you differently. In a Physique class they will look at you and your body and look at your muscles . . . Whereas in a Figure/fitness class they will look at you like a piece of meat. The way I would like to look would be the Figure but you don't want the jeering and the 'Oh my god, look at the boobs on her' . . . it's so derogatory.

For Sandra, therefore, to build a Physique body would be masculinising herself but to display her Figure/fitness body in competition would be sexually objectifying herself. Neither is acceptable to her. In contrast, Helen construes Figure/fitness as being a much more challenging task than competing in a Physique category because not only do her muscles have to be toned and defined, she also has to look 'perfect'.

A Ms Superfitness was introduced to the Ms Olympia in 1995 with the stated aim of broadening the sport and making it more accessible to a larger audience. According to Ndalianis (1995,) Joe Weider (Chairman of the IFBB) believes that having the Physique category alone is discouraging for many women who cannot, or do not wish to, achieve that much muscularity and will certainly not encourage women to take up weight training as they fear looking like the Physique bodybuilder. One has to ask, however, who the intended market really is because although Weider's stated position above implies it is women, the practice of this competition category strongly indicates that it is men. According to Sandra, the growing popularity of Figure/fitness competition is amongst men as this is entertainment for them (perhaps analogous to boxing matches where women in bikinis appear between rounds).

> That's what sells the tickets. That's the way Federations are going . . . they want more and more women to be doing Figure because the men want to come down there. It's almost like page three. They [page three girls] are there but without being topless . . . because that is what men want to see.

Sandra is certainly not alone in her view as many in the bodybuilding world consider the Figure/fitness woman as 'girlie entertainment' (Heywood, 1998; p. 30). In a letter in the March 1996 issue of *Flex* magazine, in response to the question of whether female bodybuilders or fitness competitors are sexier, the writer asks:

> Allow me to rephrase that [the question]: 'Who is sexier: an athlete or a *Playboy* model? Is Martina Navratilova or Jackie Joyner-Kersee sexier than Anna Nicole Smith?' I am sure that both of the aforementioned world champion athletes, whose goals are to defeat all comers, couldn't care less!
>
> (cited in Heywood, 1998; p. 30)

It is the bodybuilder, therefore, who is the serious athlete, not the Figure/fitness competitor. This can also be seen in a recent bodybuilding magazine discussion of attributes that make the perfect Figure/fitness woman. The following were put forward:

> Some are obvious – like an incredibly symmetrical, bountiful body. Others are subtle – like a special personality quirk, or *a glance that's erotic and innocent* [my italics] at the same time.
>
> (*All Natural Muscular Development*, September 1997; p. 96)

Would male bodybuilders be referred to in this way? This was followed by 38 pages of pin ups of the magazine's '20 Best Fitness Women' who were all described as 'the stuff of dreams and fantasies – the earth bound angels we quite frankly can't help but adore' (p. 142). Readers were invited to vote for their favourite. Presumably these readers are men because I doubt very much this magazine aims to cater for lesbians' dreams and fantasies.

The beauty and the beast

If the female bodybuilder is the serious athlete, this begs the question why more and more bodybuilding organisations are holding Figure/fitness contests and phasing out Physique contests. The IFBB recently reduced the Ms Olympia prize money from $115,000 to $60,000 whilst, at the same time raising the Fitness Olympia prize from $25,000 to $60,000 (Heywood, 1998). Although the IFBB later restored the Ms Olympia prize money, it is clear that the Physique competition is under threat. It is also clear that the Figure/fitness category has become more popular as the Physique women have become more muscular.[4]

Any analysis of women's bodybuilding must be viewed in the wider context of what bodybuilding as a whole represents and not just what it means to the people who participate. Klein (1993) reminds us that bodybuilding is a sport historically based on a male need for increased size, a sport that was founded on men and their insecurities to reinforce gender conventions. Bodybuilding, therefore, is construed by society as a way of validating notions of masculinity through muscularity and reinforcing gender conventions by enhancing what Holmlund (1989) calls 'visible difference'. Even when people find images of the male bodybuilder repulsive, my discussions with them as an academic, as a female bodybuilder and as an exercise instructor tell me that this is not because his masculinity is in question. It is simply because his hypermuscularity is considered too extreme and unattractive. Thus, as Kuhn (1988) has proposed, the male bodybuilder challenges the naturalness of the body but the female bodybuilder challenges this *plus* the natural order of gender. Whilst images of the muscular male pose no conflicts between sex and gender – it is the natural order of things – images of the muscular female are a different matter altogether. As Helen, the gym instructor and aspiring Figure/fitness competitor mentioned earlier, puts it:

> I've got nothing against women bodybuilders, if that's what they want to do, if they can. Men, I think it looks good. I think that's how a man should look. A man is a man, he's supposed to be the domineering one, at least he should have the muscle and everything. Women, I don't know. You're drawing a fine line really between women bodybuilders and men – they're identical really.

Images of the muscular woman, therefore, conflict with the associations of men as strong and women as weak that underpin gender roles and power relations in society (Holmlund, 1989). Because gender roles are familiar and comforting (to both women and men), visible femininity (i.e. the lack of it) becomes the focus in the female bodybuilder. Furthermore, Schulze (1986) contends that male sexual interest in the muscular female implies homosexuality. The female bodybuilder, therefore, is a threat, not only because she is

60

unnatural but because she has the power to invert normal male sexuality (Schulze, 1986). Thus, through enforced visible femininity, her body is safely positioned as a site of heterosexuality (Hall, 1996). She is made safe by being allowed to partake only if she knows her place – that of sexual object, there to serve male desire. Thus, according to Ndalianis (1995), the female bodybuilder has been placed in a position where she is less threatening – even if she is muscular – because in this way she caters 'to male fantasies and per-versions that play on phallic women narratives' (p. 18).

Perhaps, with the increased muscularity of the Physique women, greater efforts are required to prevent a diminishing of visible difference. Perhaps, too, as greater numbers of women have taken to training with weights, the increasing popularity of the Figure/fitness competitions reflects an accom-modation of this social change together with resistance towards it in a similar manner to the media's accommodation and resistance of sports-women (Chapter 3, this volume). Thus, so that women know their place in this world of hypermasculinity, subordination is further reinforced by taking the female bodybuilding competition closer to the traditional beauty pageant event. As Bolin (1992) has argued, the 'beast' challenges male privilege but the 'beauty' sustains it.

Advocates of Figure/fitness view these competitions as a more realistic reflection of what the average woman wants to look like and what the aver-age man wants to see in her (Heywood, 1998). Many Physique competitors are switching to Figure/fitness because they know it will be easier to market themselves and get sponsorship and recognition. Maybe also it is clearer what is expected of them in competition as there is no debate amongst judges about whether the Figure/fitness body is feminine. Perhaps, therefore, the Figure/fitness category has, as Joe Weider wishes, encouraged more women into the arena of competitive bodybuilding providing more women with greater choice. But is this really greater choice and why are men not being offered this? I am not convinced the male bodybuilder is any more a realistic reflection of what the average man wants to look like than the Physique woman is of what the average woman wants to look like. Moreover, discussions about what the average woman (or man) looks like are just not relevant in a sports context. It would be ridiculous to discuss whether the world record for the 100 metre sprint is a true reflection of how fast the average person wants to run. Yet this is what is occurring with the sport of female bodybuilding where, to make it acceptable, it has become equated with sexual attractiveness, with female bodybuilders being 'cor-rected to cultural norms' (Heywood, 1998; p. 35). Is this true choice? For Jennifer, it was not:

> As I sat in my trainer's house after competing in my first body-building competition, a magazine was placed in front of me. I was shown centerfolds of fitness competitors with tight bodies, big

breasts and long hair; and women wearing sequinned thong bikinis, high heels and a lot of makeup. My training partner at the time said: 'You don't want to be in bodybuilding, putting on that much muscle doesn't look good on a woman. That's not really your goal anyway. This is the body you want to have, isn't it?' I felt as if I had gone from working as an athlete to being persuaded to creating a body like Fitness Barbie's.

(Michalenok, 1999)

As Heywood (1998) asks: 'is this really all women are, all women can be?'

Notes

1 Powerlifting and weightlifting differ in the type of lifts and the techniques used.
2 Because of this, there is a continuing debate about whether bodybuilding is actually a sport or a performance art. It is not an Olympic sport for women or men but regional, national and world championships are overseen by organisations such as the National Amateur Bodybuilders Association (NABBA) and the English Federation of Bodybuilders (EFBB) in the UK and the International Federation of Bodybuilders (IFBB) worldwide.
3 Readers may remember Ben Johnson's humiliation of being stripped of his gold medal when he tested positive for anabolic steroid use at the 1988 Seoul Olympics. This incident brought the use of performance enhancement drugs amongst athletes very much to the attention of the public.
4 Male bodybuilders have also become more muscular, reflecting performance achievements comparable with other sports, but there are no moves afoot to limit their development.

5

THE EXERCISING WOMAN

It is not just in the world of bodybuilding, or sport in general, where women are being corrected to cultural norms. Cultural analyses have revealed that nearly every civilisation has sought to impose a uniform shape upon the female form and what this ideal is changes over time (Fallon, 1994). During the seventeenth century, when women in Western cultures were legally men's property, the ideal body was a larger well-rounded one, symbolising a well-fed woman in times of food scarcity (this is still the case in poorer cultures (Grogan, 1999)). This was an indication of a husband's or father's wealth and status. In Western cultures today, where food is plentiful and lifestyles are increasingly sedentary, the slender body has become a symbol of control, of success and of personal worthiness (Sparkes, 1997). Moreover, in the latter part of the twentieth century, this ideal body beautiful, which is held up for women to aspire to, appears to have gradually become thinner. A generation ago, the average model weighed 8% less than the average American woman, whereas the 1990s model weighs 23% less (Wolf, 1990). Between 1967 and 1987, English models' body shapes tended towards smaller breasts and narrower hips (Morris et al, 1989). This narrower hip trend has also been found in *Playboy* centrefold models (Mazur, 1986; Wiseman et al, 1992) and in the measurements of women who win Miss America contests (Wiseman et al, 1992) whose weight, incidentally, also decreased between 1979 and 1988. Alongside this increasing thinness of women held up as ideal, according to actuarial data, is an increase of 5–6 pounds in the average weight of the woman under 30 years (Garner and Garfinkel, 1980). Furthermore, we can see by simply looking around us that women's bodies come in a variety of shapes and sizes which are far removed from the media images of the ideal (usually white) woman with a much thinner body than her seventeenth century counterpart. Indeed, 42% of British women are a size 16 or more (Hargreaves, 1994).

Historical analysis has also shown that many women, over the centuries, have gone to great lengths to achieve the body beautiful of the time and this continues today. From Chinese footbinding that hindered walking to corsets that hindered breathing, today's diet industry continues to boom with a host of foods, drinks and drugs that purport to aid weight loss. Cosmetic surgery also appears to be on the increase (Thomas, 1990). Once reserved for the rich and middle aged, it has now extended to the young and the not so rich. According to a recent article in the American magazine *Newsweek*, cosmetic surgery has increased 153% since 1992, with 10 times more women than men undergoing these procedures (Kalb, 1999).

Pursuing beauty through exercise

In addition to dietary aids and cosmetic surgery, physical exercise has also become a commodity in the highly commercialised beauty culture (Morse, 1988). This initially came about as a result of an increasing acceptance of physical exercise as a desirable health behaviour in the latter part of the twentieth century (Chapter 1, this volume) and can be seen in Wiseman et al's (1992) survey of six American women's magazines[1] over a 30 year period. They found a significant increase in the number of diet, exercise and diet/exercise articles with the number of exercise articles surpassing diet articles in 1981. Exercise/diet articles (defined as articles that focussed on both diet and exercise as a combined weight loss programme) also increased markedly around that time. The influence of exercise then resulted in changed ideas of what the body beautiful should look like. In the 1970s when the fitness boom began, the body beautiful was thin and soft and curvy. Women were encouraged to exercise but discouraged from developing muscles (Markula, 1995). However, as the exercise trend continued, this attitude changed, particularly in the 1980s with the publication of *Jane Fonda's Workout Book* in 1981. Her muscle tone led to the chic and the athletic image of femininity becoming the highly desirable body beautiful (Bordo, 1990). This trend has continued to the extent that for the 1990s woman, the perfect, healthy body is not just thin, it is firm, well toned and sexy (Hall, 1996). Sagginess or wrinkling, even on a thin body, is not beautiful.

There is significant potential, therefore, for women's participation in physical activity to be influenced by this modern day body beautiful and indeed, this is borne out in the considerable psychological research that has examined motivational factors for exercise (see Biddle, 1995). Over the years this research has shown that both women and men report exercising for a number of reasons but more women than men report weight control and physical appearance as reasons (Canada Fitness Survey, 1983; ADNFS, 1992; Markland and Hardy, 1993; Davis et al, 1995). For some women this weight control appears to be the primary reason, as Penny, a participant in Maguire and Mansfield's (1998) ethnographic study of aerobic exercise classes, explained:

> Ultimately, I do exercise for weight reasons . . . I hate my legs and my bum and my arms, because they are really horrible and fat . . . I

go to the gym every day . . . I wouldn't want to stop . . . If I was really thin, I don't think I'd go at all.

(Maguire and Mansfield, 1998; p. 129)

And from Drew's (1996a) study of motivations to exercise:

I exercise if I need it at the time – depending on whether I am diet-ing or not . . . if I was lovely and slim I wouldn't be obliged to go and do any [exercise] and that is it really. Partly the health benefit that I could improve my figure.

(Drew, 1996a; p. 63)

From this quote it would appear that health and thinness have become syn-onymous, with physical exercise being constructed as a way to achieve this. Thus, beauty related weight loss has become equated with health and it is this that provides the motivation to take part in physical exercise. Similar findings emerged in one of our studies where women were interviewed about what health and exercise meant to them (Dean and Choi, 1996). Again health was associated with being thin and the person who exercised was seen as both of these: 'The image of the exerciser goes together with the healthy image, the slim or toned body' (Dean and Choi, 1996; p. 31).

This has become very apparent to me through discussions with women at sports centres, gymnasia and other exercise settings. 'Why are you here when you are not fat?' is a question that I am frequently asked. (Incidentally, most of the women who ask me this are not fat either but seem to be imply-ing that they are.) When this question was casually put to my friend and colleague Nanette Mutrie and me by a group of women in the changing room of a sports centre, we asked them if weight control was the only reason they exercised. Initially they responded yes but on further reflection told us that it was also good for stress management. It would seem, there-fore, that physical exercise is seen primarily as a beauty activity instead of a health activity.

Beauty equals health

Examination of the ways that exercise is promoted to women reveals how exercise is portrayed as a beauty activity under the guise of a healthy activ-ity. Instead of advocating exercise as a means of improving physical and psychological health, it is instead promoted as a way of losing weight and improving muscle tone and appearance. For example, Duncan's (1994) qual-itative analysis of the American health and fitness magazine *Shape* describes the regular inclusion of success stories of women who had improved their bodies. Instead of reporting resting heart rate, cholesterol levels and blood pressure – the true indicators of health and fitness – measurements of bust size, hips, waist, pounds and percentage body fat lost were given. As changes in some of these measurements have little to do with fitness or health, Duncan (1994) suggests that the aim of the magazine is to deceive the reader into believing that it is inch loss that will lead to improved health. She asks:

> Why else would *Shape* document these measurements? Furthermore, these charts invite the reader to compare her measurements to those of the model. The implicit message: How well do YOU measure up, compared to our healthy, lovely model?
>
> (Duncan, 1994; pp. 55–56)

This is still the case in 1999 where these success stories remain a regular feature of the magazine. Moreover, other articles that do discuss exercising for fitness and sport (in *Shape* and in a variety of other British and American magazines that I have scrutinised) continue to give weight loss and appearance the primary emphasis. For example, in the *Shape* September 1999 issue an article recommending weight training exercises for improved sports performance is preceded with:

> Your ultimate body. These 8 smart moves will not only rev your metabolism and burn more calories, they'll also build your best-performing – and greatest-looking body ever.
>
> (*Shape*, September 1999; pp. 114–121)

Another article in the same issue (Fit for a millennium: Y2K solutions for a 1999 body, pp. 92–99) lists the following as the top seven fitness goals for the new millennium, not all of which are indicators of fitness (those that are are marked with an asterisk):

1. Taut defined abs
2. Sculpted arms and shoulders
3. Improved muscle strength* and tone
4. Increased flexibility*
5. Lean legs and a firm butt
6. Enhanced cardiovascular stamina*
7. Weight loss*

Duncan (1994) points out the assumption of *Shape* magazine that women's bodies are flawed and that every woman should try to improve. An invitation to reshape their bodies is extended to all readers, not just those who are overweight or unshapely, and this is well illustrated in the seven fitness goals above that emphasise an improved appearance as much as fitness. In particular, *Shape* does not point out that weight loss (Goal 7 above) should only be for those individuals who actually are overweight.

Furthermore, Goal 6 is promoted as a calorie burning mechanism which it is, of course, but it is also a cholesterol, blood pressure and resting heart rate reducing mechanism. Nowhere in the article is this mentioned.

This assumption that all women's bodies are flawed is not just restricted to *Shape* magazine nor is it just restricted to magazines. Monica recounted to me her story of joining a new gym where it was assumed without question that she was there to lose weight and inches. She had, in fact, upon turning 40 years of age, become concerned about heart disease and osteoporosis. She therefore decided that it was high time to improve her health and get fitter and stronger so that she will have good quality of life as she gets older. She joined a gym and at her introductory session the exercise instructor insisted on weighing Monica and measuring her body fat level. Monica was unhappy about this because she had avoided exercise previously due to anxiety about her body. Having overcome this to the point of actually joining the gym she felt that knowing these measures would turn her focus back to what her body looked like, so she refused. Monica told me that the instructor was amazed and asked her how she would be able to tell if she was making any progress without these measurements. As Monica's goals were not to lose weight but to improve her health and fitness the answer of course is with measures such as resting heart rate, blood pressure, cardiovascular fitness and muscle strength and flexibility but these were not on offer. It was body weight and body fat or nothing. Monica conceded but asked to not be told what her measurements were. To measure her own progress she had, at the time I spoke to her, decided to focus on her increasing strength and muscle development as she continued with her new exercise programme. She told me: 'I want a pair of biceps by the time I'm 50. That's my goal.'

Women's imperfect bodies

Not only will inch loss improve health, it is also portrayed as a way to improve life. It is well established that overweight children and adults are considered to be less personable, less attractive, less popular and in poorer psychological health (Tiggemann and Rothblum, 1988) and these negative stereotypes are also held by overweight people themselves. We are told that weight loss will guard against this as is indicated by the two success stories in the September 1999 issue of *Shape* magazine. One of the successful women claims that 'for the first time in my life, I feel beautiful' (p. 72) and the other reports 'I'm the happiest I've ever been' (p. 74). Moreover, consider this extract from *Shape* magazine analysed as part of Markula's (1995) ethnographic study of the aerobics sub-culture:

> If you balk at pool-party invitations; if you lie awake at night wondering how to cover your thighs while keeping cool and looking

great; if you seriously consider moving to Antarctica as soon as the hot weather sets in – this workout is for you.

(cited in Markula, 1995; p. 434)

This voice of liberation – endless pool parties without worry – masks a control of women by a patriarchal society where the body is always imperfect. To perfect the body it is fragmented into problem parts such as stomach, thighs, bottoms and under-arms and special exercises in order to tone them are recommended (Markula, 1995; Maguire and Mansfield, 1998). For example, in the *Shape* September 1999 issue special exercises were recommended for the under-arms (Do it right: shape the back of your arms with a classic exercise) and the bottom (One on One: great glutes can be yours with these three exercises). British *Zest* magazine promotes martial arts as a form of exercise to improve your body (Kick Butt! And get a flat stomach, November 1999). The British version of *Shape* recommends a dance move for the bottom (Do it right: the arabasque reach – a powerful dance move to tone your bottom, October 1999). And, Workout: walk your way to thinner thighs (*Rosemary Conley's Diet and Fitness* magazine, October/November 1999).

Aerobic exercise classes such as aerobic dance, step aerobics, body conditioning, keep fit, to name but a few (hereafter generically called aerobics) also usually include exercises especially for these 'problem areas'. Indeed, there are whole exercise classes devoted to them such as the hugely popular 'tums, bums and thighs' classes. The advertising of aerobics videos for home use also emphasises that the exercises will address these problem areas. Consider the promotional text of two exercise videos produced by *Cosmopolitan* magazine that were advertised in the March 1994 UK issue:

The latest fat-burning cardiovascular step challenge! Plus a fantastic toning section for a flatter stomach and a trimmer waist.

(*Cosmopolitan Step Workout* video, UK National Magazine Company)

The ultimate body toning workout to firm your stomach, tone your thighs and shape up your bustline.

(*Cosmopolitan Tonetics* video)

Thus, instead of being promoted to both women and men as a way of improving the cardiovascular system, bone density, muscular strength and flexibility – all health benefits of physical exercise – these videos are promoted to women as a way of losing weight and improving sex appeal. A third *Cosmopolitan* video reinforces this with: 'Cardiovascular workouts for a healthy, sexy body' (The great body shape tape).

Of course participation guarantees cardiovascular benefits even if this is not the primary motive. It could, therefore, be asked why it matters if the end result will be the same. After all, according to the British magazine *Rosemary Conley's Diet and Fitness*, 'good old straightforward walking is the best activity to give you thinner thighs and a pear shape can literally transform her legs with a regular programme' (p. 32, October/November 1999) but the article does go on to list secondary benefits such as reduced blood pressure, cholesterol and risk of osteoporosis too. Thus, as one exercise guru says of aerobics: 'they [women] go to the programme to improve their looks and they get fitness and health as fringe benefits' (Cooper, 1970; p. 134).

One reason why it matters is that research into motivation to exercise has shown us that unrealistic goals are more likely to lead to drop out (Biddle and Mutrie, 1991). It is noteworthy that, as Duncan (1994) points out, some of the so-called 'problem areas' that require reshaping happen to be some of those that biologically distinguish women from men. Optimum female reproductive function requires sufficient levels of body fat and women are biologically predisposed to store this fat in the breasts, hips, thighs and stomach areas. Consistently being told that these areas are problematic leads to dissatisfaction with the female form (Bordo, 1990). But perhaps that is the aim because this will encourage women to exercise and the fitness industry, like the diet industry, can continue to be profitable even though the flat stomach and narrow hip look is more synonymous with the body of a young boy and because we are women, most of us will not be able to attain this body beautiful, regardless of how hard we try – most women are just not born with slim, lean, boy shaped bodies. Duncan (1994) reminds us that even fashion models have not achieved the ideal body – their photographs are altered using computer imaging because even *they* are not beautiful enough. Moreover, the physiological evidence suggests that it is not possible to lose fat in a very specific area by working the underlying group of muscles (Sharkey, 1990). The 'tums, bums and thighs' class, therefore, is not as effective as its marketing would have us believe and the goal of reducing these areas through specific exercises is unrealistic. Women, therefore, through the beauty equals health discourse, are being set up for failure in terms of achieving the body beautiful (Duncan, 1994). Thus, whilst exercise for beauty might encourage some women to exercise, this is not likely to lead to long-term adherence, which is what is required for the true health benefits to be realised.

Reducing the body

In her ethnographic study of the aerobics sub-culture, Markula (1995) found that when asked to identify any problematic parts of their bodies, the women's answers reflected the discourse of women's imperfect bodies. For example, one of Markula's research participants confirmed that she and others exercised because they felt their bodies had flaws:

> I think everyone there has a certain area that they want to work on; it's obvious to them or it's obvious to you, they wouldn't be there if they hadn't a complex about [some area]. They don't like some- thing . . . like a stereotype, we don't like our arms, that's why we signed up . . . we are trying to get rid of our arms.
>
> (Markula, 1995; p. 434)

Similar findings emerged from Maguire and Mansfield's (1998) study where one participant explained that 'there are lots of women here who are trying to lose weight . . . to get rid of this or that bit of fat or lose their tummy' (p. 125). This discourse of reducing, or getting rid of the body has also been identified in discursive constructions of the anorexic body (Malson, 1999). In this study participants talked about their bodies as disappearing bodies: 'It's just a way of like trying to disappear'; 'I just wanted to fade away'; 'I remember sort of looking in the mirror and actually being surprised that I saw a form in the mirror and not just a nothingness' (Malson, 1999; p. 145). Malson (1999) proposes that the disappearing body is a postmodern construction based on our consumer culture where the body is always imper- fect but, at the same time, is perfectible by working to achieve 'the look'. The achievement of this 'look' is emphasised not just in the aerobics class but within the whole exercise for beauty sub-culture. For example, in maga- zines and books providing exercise 'tips' or instruction, extreme muscularity is discouraged because this symbolises strength and masculinity (Bordo, 1990; Chapter 4, this volume). Muscularity would increase, not reduce, the body so American *Heart and Soul* magazine explains how to 'make muscles without the bulk' (August 1999) in an article entitled 'Fitness for everybody: you can lift weights without getting bulky'. Readers are introduced to Edie, Jan and Tomeka who 'move heavy metal in the gym, but there is clearly nothing "mannish" or "bulky" about them' (p. 52; photographs of the women accompany the article). In the article we learn that it is unlikely that lifting weights will make women appear masculine. Jan, a personal trainer who can push 320 pounds on the leg press machine and bench press 135 pounds, explains that she lifts weights because: 'With more muscle than fat, I burn more calories. It also shapes your body better than anything else going' (p. 53). Thus, muscles give your body shape and are promoted as a way of losing weight because the body with muscle tone burns more calories at rest than the body without. As Betty Weider advises in her 'Body by Betty' column in *Muscle and Fitness* magazine:

> [weight training is] just as integral to your exercise programme as cardio. Weight training increases lean muscle mass, which actually

boosts your metabolism, since muscle itself burns calories. Lifting will also shape and tighten your body, giving you a firmer, more defined look.

(*Muscle and Fitness*, October 1999; p. 176)

Muscularity is also promoted as a way of making you look smaller. For example, broad shoulders will make your waist appear smaller and toned arms will make your arms appear smaller because they will be tight, not flabby. And for Jan, the personal trainer featured in *Heart and Soul*: 'the heavier I've lifted, the smaller and leaner I've gotten – especially around the hips' (*Heart and Soul*, August 1999; p. 53). Strength exercises, therefore, are used to reduce women's bodies as dieting does. Considered by Markula's research participants to be 'tortuous, hard and horrible', they were necessary, not to strengthen the body in order to be more physically able but to reduce the body to look more like the ideal.

Because of this need to reduce the body, to be thin, in Markula's (1995) ethnographic study of the aerobics sub-culture, weight loss was much more important for the research participants than muscle tone. An extreme example of this was one research participant who took part in many other activities as well as aerobics. She particularly enjoyed ice-hockey, which develops leg muscles, so to counteract this, she did not eat:

You have 50 pounds of equipment [when you play ice-hockey] and you go skating around, it's going to build up my muscles unless I don't eat anything.

(Markula, 1995; p. 440)

The dilemma for this woman, therefore, is that to play ice-hockey muscular size and strength are needed (as well as sufficient energy from food) but she must also reduce her body size in order to look feminine so she denies herself food to achieve this.

Body dissatisfaction

Another reason why exercising for beauty matters is that this environment, where the body is always imperfect, may foster fault finding with one's own body as a result of the emphasis on appearance (Davis, 1997). This could be the case irrespective of whether the woman's original motive for exercising was health or beauty and even if she is generally satisfied with her body. For example, Krane et al's (1998) qualitative study of exercisers and athletes found that every woman expressed concern about some area(s) of their bodies that needed improvement, even when they were generally satisfied: 'For the most part I'm happy, but like I'm always striving to be better and always trying to lose weight.'

Krane et al (1998) contend that this particular explanation reflected the views of the other participants very well:

> I have areas that I could be more happy with, but there are areas of me that I don't know if I'm necessarily proud of, but happy with. I know that I have worked hard to get my body in good shape and there are areas that are toned and defined and everything else. It kind of reassures me, makes me happy to go 'yes!' when I look in the mirror. But then there's other [body parts], you know . . . there are some areas that I would definitely like to improve upon.

Thus, one scenario in the exercise for beauty environment is that while the woman may come to be more satisfied with (parts of) her body shape as her muscles get toned, she may simultaneously become less satisfied with her overall weight or with certain body parts as her ideal shifts towards a thinner/less fat/more toned standard. This may be particularly the case when the comparator is the thin, toned lycra clad woman exemplified by aerobic exercise instructors and indeed, many other women in the aerobics class. Maguire and Mansfield's ethnographic study of the aerobics sub-culture revealed the existence of an 'established group' within the class who were the regular attenders, working at the front of the class, in their leotards, providing a '"chorus line" of tanned, toned breasts, bottoms, legs and backs . . . Setting the standards of appearance' (Maguire and Mansfield, 1998; p. 121). Those who did not have the body beautiful (and/or were not yet competent at performing the movements?) worked at the back of the class in teeshirts and leggings or tracksuit bottoms which are not as revealing of their bodies as leotards.

If it is the case that exercise encourages a negative attitude towards the body, one would expect this to be evident from studies of the relationship between exercise and body satisfaction. The findings of this primarily quantitative research, however, are very mixed, with most studies finding no relationship between frequency of exercise and body satisfaction in young and middle-aged women and little or no relationship with weight preoccupation although commitment to exercise is positively related to weight and diet concerns (Davis, 1997). Clearly there are methodological concerns to consider here such as measurement issues and research designs that are cross-sectional or correlational (e.g. how does one know whether the research participants were satisfied or dissatisfied with their bodies prior to the exercise programme). In particular, it is apparent from the qualitative research data presented here that body image is a complex phenomenon. One can be satisfied and not satisfied simultaneously as is depicted in the quotes from Krane et al's (1998) study. Thus, psychometric measures that assume body satisfaction and body dissatisfaction to be opposite ends of a continuum are not the most appropriate way of assessing how one feels about one's body. Indeed, innovative research into weight concern by Kate Bennett (1995) found through repertory grid technique that thin and fat are not opposite ends of a continuum. Bennett's (1995) research participants, who were both eating disordered and non-eating disordered women, were not striving to be thin, but to be not fat. Bennett (1995) concluded that 'eating disorders can be regarded, not as a drive to thinness, but as a flight from fatness' (p. 129).

It would be intriguing to ascertain whether similar findings would emerge from research into different physical exercise contexts. It certainly seems that when the comparators are not thin, toned and lycra clad, and/or when the objective of the physical activity is not to improve the body, the woman can feel very differently about her body in that setting. This was seen in a recent study of a group of Western women learning Middle Eastern dance and a group of contemporary dance performers (Hanley, 1999). Sometimes referred to as belly dancing, curvaceous hips and a rounded stomach are positively valued for the kinds of movement required in Middle Eastern dance. Therefore, when dancing, one research participant did not feel negative about her stomach but this was not, however, mirrored outside of this setting:

> This thing of fat that we have in Western society, that fat is bad, I only feel when I wear Western clothes . . . [In Middle Eastern costume] I'd feel fine about my tummy coming out, being round, whereas if I wear jeans, there's a 'control yourself' sort of thing.
> (Hanley, 1999)

A similar finding emerged from another participant, a contemporary dance performer, who describes how this type of dance, as a physical activity concerned with movement, enables her to have a positive body image:

> when I think about my body through dance, it's very positive and growthful . . . it's a good sense of body image through thinking about movement. However, if I walk out and I'm not thinking about dance or I'm not thinking through that way, but more through 'out there' and what's expected of me, I have a very poor self image.
> (Hanley, 1999)

Self-objectification

From these women's experiences, it can be seen how different activity contexts can have different effects on how the body is experienced and how general (Western) societal pressures concerning the body beautiful can remain intact outside of those contexts. This can be explained by objectification theory which, following Berger (1972), contends that 'our culture socialises girls and women to internalise an objectifying observer's perspective on their bodies' (Fredrickson et al, 1998; p. 270). This occurs through the greater sexual objectification of women than men and has the effect of self-objectification where the woman learns to view her body from the perspective of how others see her. Another example is the athletes in Krane et al's (1998) study, who, as with the dancers above, were highly satisfied with their bodies as athletes because they were strong, powerful and skilful and in that context, that is what is expected. However, they were well aware that their strong muscular bodies were not congruent with the societal ideal body beautiful and, in social settings outside of the sport context, the women felt that they were too muscular and feared being considered masculine looking. Self-objectification can also occur inside the sporting context, however, when, as we have seen in the previous chapters, the script of archetypal femininity is imposed upon the female athlete and bodybuilder. As discussed, when attempts are made to feminise the sportswoman through, for example, clothing that emphasises sexual objectification, she is reminded that her body is subjected to the gaze of others.

Duncan (1994) uses Foucault's (1979) panopticon metaphor to illustrate how self-objectification can occur in the exercise for beauty setting. The panopticon is a prison structure where the guard is positioned in a tower at its centre with the prisoners positioned all around. This arrangement ensures that the guard can see all the prisoners but they cannot see the guard and do not know whether they are being observed. However, the mere possibility of observation ensures compliance through the prisoners acting as their own observer. Scholars such as Bartky (1990) and Bordo (1989) argue that in an analogous way, women have become the observers and monitors of their own bodies by turning the panoptic gaze upon themselves. Duncan (1994) suggests that the panoptic gaze occurs in the exercise for beauty setting through the use of various, what she terms, panoptic mechanisms such as the assumption that every woman's body is flawed and in need of improvement and the subordination of health issues to beauty issues. She argues that 'Disguised as health, beauty becomes a worthy, achievable, private goal, one engaged in for its own sake. If one fails to attain this exalted form of health, then one has only oneself to blame' (Duncan, 1994; p. 57).

Furthermore, the panoptic gaze is a masculine gaze where heterosexual feminine appropriateness is salient. For example, in Markula's (1995) study, great concern was expressed by the research participants about being too muscular and looking masculine. Having muscular arms was perceived as masculine but muscular legs (not too muscular of course!) were considered more socially acceptable and sought after because it was believed that men noticed them, unlike arms:

> The thing that guys look at or a lot of women are concerned, tends to be your butt or their thighs. They don't say, 'I have fat arms' . . .

and you don't have guys going by and saying 'Look at those sexy arms'.

(Markula, 1995; p. 436)

Thus, well-toned legs are desirable because this is believed to be desirable to men and although most of the women in Markula's study felt they needed more muscle tone in their upper bodies too, they preferred doing their legs – presumably because this was deemed of more interest to men. Interestingly, comparisons of women's and men's preferred female bodies found that women believe men to prefer thinner bodies than men themselves report preferring although men's preferences were still thinner than women's perceptions of their own weight (Fallon and Rozin, 1985; Lamb et al, 1993).

The concern of the women in Markula's study with what men think about their body parts, which was also evident in Maguire and Mansfield's (1998) study, illustrates two points. First, it illustrates how the women, in discussing their bodies, do so through the panoptic gaze – i.e. through the eyes of others as posited by self-objectification theory (Fredrickson et al, 1998). Second, it illustrates how, due to the influence of compulsive heterosexuality the 'others' through which the woman sees herself is the masculine gaze.

Feminine appropriate exercise

Yet another reason why exercising for beauty matters is that in this environment where the body is always imperfect there is little opportunity to take pride in attaining the real health benefits of exercise. For example, one woman in Markula's ethnographic study felt pride and shame simultaneously in her increased physical strength:

> It is really contradictory, because the very things that I do in aerobics, like my class always has this long session of push-ups, I'm strong and I feel uncomfortable with that, but at the same time I'm proud of that, not proud, that makes me feel good about myself to be strong, but I don't know.

(Markula, 1995; p. 439)

This sense of contradiction stems from the current ideal of the feminine body that is slim and toned, not strong, and the traditional notions of gender that equate strength with masculinity, not femininity. Thus, in the context of beauty related exercise, physical activity has become acceptable for women in order to reduce their bodies; to limit perceptions of the female body and to perpetuate patriarchal notions of femininity where the woman is smaller and takes up less space, is more passive and weaker than men (Hargreaves, 1994). Aerobics classes, in particular, are an acceptable way for women to be physically active – feminine appropriate – but according to Maguire and Mansfield (1998) are 'more oppressive than liberating for women' (p. 129). This is firstly because in the environment where exercise is undertaken to improve the imperfect body in order to look more beautiful and not to strengthen it in order to be more physically able, there is little pride to be had in the increased strength that inevitably occurs. This is not empowering. Secondly, the beauty equals health discourse ensures women's failure in attaining the body beautiful. In disempowering women, their bodies remain controlled and so does their behaviour as time, money and energy spent in the pursuit of beauty means women have fewer resources to fight the inequalities inherent in a patriarchal society. Furthermore, women's bodies are used to enhance visible differences and maintain the gender order of society (see Chapter 4, this volume) through a physical activity that is performed to ensure the body remains according to traditional notions of femininity – small and without muscularity. This is true too of men who appear, in greater numbers than previously, to be motivated to exercise in order to improve their bodies (Pope et al, 2000). In keeping with patriarchal notions of masculinity, their goal is usually to build larger muscles. Men, therefore, continue to dominate the gym whilst women dominate the aerobics class (Maguire and Mansfield, 1998). However, as Duncan (1994) points out, whilst the Arnold Schwartznegger body may be as unattainable to the average man as the slim, toned ideal is to women, (heterosexual) men's worth is not as tied to their appearance as (heterosexual) women's is. The importance of measuring up and the damaging consequences of failure, therefore, are far greater for women than for men.

Empowering women

Empowerment is a term often associated with sport and physical exercise and refers to 'the confident sense of self that comes from being skilled in the use of one's body' (Whitson, 1994; p. 354). Sport and physical exercise are key areas (previously reserved for men) which have allowed women access to success and expression of bodily strength and skill. However, in accommodating this social change, resistance occurs simultaneously in the construction of exercise as a beauty product. I contend, therefore, that in motivating women to exercise for beauty reasons, there is greater opportunity for disempowerment than empowerment and in such a predominantly beauty related exercise culture it is not always easy for women to find alternative exercise discourses. (This also applies to our wider society and the objectification of women.) Moreover, the dominant discourse of beauty might actually discourage women from exercising and this is yet another reason to be concerned about exercise as a beauty product. As one woman who regularly exercises but chooses not to categorise herself as an exerciser told us:

I'm no, you know, elfin type you know . . . sylph like figure or anything like this. I'm sort of like bigger . . . if I do in a way go
wholeheartedly and say 'yes I exercise, yes I'm an exerciser', in
which case people are gonna be like . . . 'but you're not exactly thin
are you?'

(Dean and Choi, 1996; p. 33)

Although this does not prevent this particular woman from exercising, it can
prevent others and this is not uncommon:

I love doing aerobics but since I changed jobs I've put on weight so
I've stopped going. I wouldn't be seen dead in a leotard.

(Drew, 1996a; p. 63)

Swimming here is a nightmare, there is definitely a negative loop in
my motivation. There's a wonderful pool in Northern California
where the women are all at least fourteen stones and it's heaven for
me. It's wonderful to feel almost thin.

(Drew, 1996a; p. 63)

Thus, alongside the belief that beauty will result from exercise, there is a
belief that one has to be beautiful in order to exercise. Once again, this is not
empowering. Yet, women can be empowered by physical activity through the
reinforcement of positive attitudes towards their bodies and a sense of power
from their physical abilities (Theberge, 1987). For example, a number of
women in Markula's study did not exercise for beauty reasons, but to be
strong and independent:

Because if I am physically strong, I can do things that I want to do:
I can unscrew jam jars – I don't have to ask some guys to do it for
me – I can put the trash out; I can lift things. I don't like feeling
weak and helpless and end up asking people to do things for me.

(Markula, 1995; p. 438)

And, from Maguire and Mansfield's (1998) study:

I like the classes so much . . . Aerobics makes me feel good and I'm
always bouncing about and walking with a spring in my step . . .
They [the classes] are so much fun, and you meet so many people.

(Arminda, p. 132)

It makes me feel great, because you can switch off and not think
about anything for a while.

(Jane, p. 132)

I find it gives me an outlet after work. It's a great way of getting rid of frustration . . . It gets rid of stress . . . I come out feeling good.

(Ruth, p. 132)

Thus, it is certainly not the case that all women who exercise or take part in sport do so for beauty reasons nor do all readers of *Shape* magazine believe their bodies to be flawed. Women are not passive dupes who simply accept the scripts of femininity. Through physical exercise women can resist them. Fun, stress relief and socialising are also motives as well as increased strength and improved health but these need to be emphasised over and above the beauty discourses so that women can truly have choice and access to the empowerment that is so rightfully theirs. A heterosexually beautiful and feminine body is not all women are or all that women can be.

Notes

1 *Harpers Bazaar, Vogue, Ladies Home Journal, Good Housekeeping, Woman's Day* and *McCalls*.

6

THE INFLUENCE OF
THE SPORTY TYPE

In the previous chapters I have illustrated how the sporty type is positioned as masculine and how within this masculine culture, women's participation is more acceptable when it is in feminine appropriate sports. I have also argued that women's sport is considered of less interest and importance than men's sport; and that sportswomen's achievements are placed secondary to their (heterosexual) feminine characteristics. I have argued that within the masculine culture of sport, women's sport has been accommodated, but at the same time resisted, through hegemonic femininity where the female athlete's body is (hetero) sexualised; where, although she is strong and independent she is subordinated and made to fit with cultural norms. This is also prevalent in the world of women's recreational physical exercise, particularly in the aerobics sub-culture, where women are encouraged to exercise according to conceptions of femininity that emphasise beauty over health. As a result, this activity which has the potential to be empowering for women by providing a women-dominated, if not women-only space to experience their physical bodies and to develop physical skills, instead limits the experience to one of sexualised physicality (Theberge, 1997). The question for this chapter is, how might the sporty type as masculine, and hegemonic femininity within women's sport and exercise, play a role, amongst other factors, in influencing girls' and women's perceptions of themselves as physically active beings and hence their physical activity choices?

School experiences

It is well established that childhood experiences are important influences on later behaviours and physical activity is no different. People who were physically active as children are far more likely to be physically active as adults (US Surgeon General, 1996). School experiences are very important in this regard because through physical education (PE), children are presented with opportunities to participate in sports. For many girls, this is their first, and possibly only, opportunity to develop physical skills and to experience their bodies in that way (McManus and Armstrong, 1996). However, as a result of gendering the school PE environment continues to reinforce the ideology of sport as a masculine domain.[1] This occurs in many ways. For example, PE has a much stronger male presence than female. There are fewer female coaches and, at secondary school level fewer female heads of PE departments (Sports Council, 1991). This of course means that there are fewer role models for girls but it also means that decisions about PE programmes continue to be based on male values and male experiences (Hargreaves, 1994). Thus, the revised British school curriculum has recently increased the emphasis given to team games and aggressive competitive activity (DfE, 1995). This further reinforces sport as a masculine domain because it offers boys, whose play behaviour is more often characterised by aggressive and competitive activities, more opportunities for physical experiences and achievement goals associated with these activities. Activities such as dance are not compulsory after the age of 11 years which means that it is likely to be excluded (Hargreaves, 1994). Indeed, male PE teachers argue that dance should not be included in the curriculum at all (Talbot, 1990a) and thus sport remains a culture that emphasises masculinity through often aggressive and competitive team sports.

In addition, considerable research has found that both male and female PE teachers tend to spend more time with and give more attention to boys (Carli, 1993). They also have stereotyped ideas of girls' physical capabilities (Scratton, 1992; Flintoff, 1993). This can result in poorer resources and facilities being made available for girls' PE, as one 15 year old reported of her school (Coakley and White, 1992). In this qualitative study to explore young people's participation in sport, the girls in this school were assigned a venue for PE that was so small there was not enough space to play any games involving physical activity. The boys, on the other hand, had a very large gym. This young woman was very clear to the researchers that the message she received from this situation was that sports were not for women.

Another result is the smaller choice of available activities for girls, as reported by Young and White (1995) who interviewed female athletes about their childhood sports experiences.

> In high school physical education, we could choose from a whole list of sports we wanted to learn. However, our teacher wouldn't permit the girls to do half of them because we were ladies and shouldn't be involved in those such as football, weight training and rugby.
> (Young and White, 1995; p. 50)

This remains the case amongst today's school girls. In a British study of adolescents conducted between September 1997 and December 1998 in order to assess the impact of recent policy on the provision of PE for adolescent girls, the same gender divisions were found to still be in place (Williams and Bedward, 1999). Sports such as soccer, rugby, cricket and basketball were not on offer to most of the girls in the study. In contrast, only netball was not on offer to the boys. Even when the school policy is to offer all activities to all children irrespective of sex the girls can still be denied the same opportunities as the boys. Williams and Bedward (1999) found that many female teachers did not feel competent to teach soccer, which was why it was not on offer to the girls. Perhaps these teachers were denied the opportunity to play soccer when they were younger and/or to develop those skills when training to be PE teachers because it was not considered feminine appropriate. If so, this further demonstrates one way in which beliefs that soccer is a male sport are inadvertently reinforced through the continuing influence of hegemonic femininity.

Many of the girls in Williams and Bedward (1999) study really enjoyed playing soccer and were frustrated that they were denied the opportunity to do so at school. They felt that as a result of this, when they played outside of school, they were less skilled than the boys with whom they played. This, of course, is another way of reinforcing the archetypal ideology of soccer as a boys' sport and that they are better at/more suited to it than girls. This can also occur even when girls are allowed to play, because of differential treatment by their coaches and, on co-ed teams, by their male team mates. This has been noted in the USA where co-ed soccer teams are common in many cities. Firstly, coaches often do not call the girls to play and leave them waiting around on the sidelines, and secondly, when they are allowed to play the boys do not pass the ball to them (Whiteside, 1997). Thus, although girls are allowed to play in theory, in practice they have less opportunity to do so. As a result, the girls' skills, not surprisingly, remain less developed than the boys – again reinforcing the old stereotypes. Hidden behind the alleged progressiveness and equal opportunity of the co-ed team gendering continues to take place. As Young and White (1995) point out, 'initial sports experiences, as with other forms of physical culture, are components of a larger gendering process' (p. 50).

Further evidence of this can be seen in issues that are unrelated to sports activities per se. For example, in Coakley and White's (1992) study, the uniform (a short skirt) that the girls and young women had to wear for PE was highly instrumental in creating a dislike of PE. This was also found almost a decade later by Williams and Bedward (1999). As well as causing embarrassment because of modesty concerns, these short skirts are a problem because in the winter it is freezing cold. One has to ask why girls and women continue to be required to wear impractical skimpy clothing for sport. The only viable answer I can come up with is hegemonic femininity. This also occurs at elite level sport where women athletes have to wear swimsuit/leotard type uniforms or bikini strips and crop tops (see Chapter 3, this volume). Arguments about aerodynamics and wind resistance just do not hold up when this is not required of male athletes. They can wear shorts and teeshirts or baggy vests. In addition, as one track and field athlete told me, these skimpy outfits are uncomfortable and impractical because they have a habit of moving around in adverse ways as the athlete moves. For example, when she pole vaulted she feared being immodestly exposed as she swung her legs up in the air and when she long jumped she often ended up with sand in her bikini bottoms, which was very uncomfortable.

Body image concerns enhanced by these skimpy uniforms have been found to negatively influence the female athlete's focus and subsequent performance (Krane et al, 1998) and in both Coakley and White's (1992) and Williams and Bedward's (1999) studies these same concerns led to PE being viewed negatively. For the same reason, showering was also a problem. In both studies, in schools where the shower facilities were communal, the girls admitted to avoiding PE because they found this very stressful. Thus, for the girls and young women in Coakley and White's (1992) study, the short skirt and the showering issues led to PE being 'associated with feelings of discomfort and embarrassment' (p. 31). In contrast, none of the boys or young men in Coakley and White's (1992) study complained about having to wear shorts, of being cold in the winter or of negative shower experiences. In addition, not many of them felt their current sports participation, or non-participation, was influenced by school experiences, but for many of the girls and young women, it was. It should, therefore, be apparent that the school sports curriculum and environment is still not adequate for girls and 'it is little wonder that we have such an inactive population of girls; we have been schooling them to be so' (McManus and Armstrong, 1996; p. 35).

Perceptions of ability

Because of the masculine culture of sport and archetypal femininity, girls and women have reduced opportunities to develop physical skills. Not surprisingly, they also have less confidence in their physical abilities than boys and men do (Corbin et al, 1983; Vealey, 1986; Feltz et al, 1989; George, 1994). Moreover, recent research has revealed that women expect to be less competent at a 'masculine' sport than a 'feminine' one but men expect to be equally competent at both (Lirgg et al, 1996). In a study of baton whirling and kung fu, 81 male and 79 female undergraduates with no prior experience of these activities were shown videos explaining and demonstrating the necessary skills. They were asked to rate how confident they felt of their ability to perform, with practice, the skills related to each task. In addition, half of the participants were told that ability to perform such skills is innate and the other half that it is learned. All of the participants rated baton whirling and kung fu to be feminine and masculine sports respectively and those who were told that ability is acquired felt more confident than those who were told it is learned. Results also revealed that women were more confident than men at baton whirling and men were more confident than women at kung fu. However, men were equally confident about baton whirling and about kung fu whereas the women were more confident about baton whirling than kung fu. This held true for the men when comparisons were made between the learned and innate groups but with the women, both the learned and innate groups were equally confident about baton twirling but not kung fu.

This may not hold true for gender neutral tasks, however. In Lirgg et al's (1996) study a large number of the original sample recruited rated kung fu as gender neutral so separate analyses were conducted on this group (N = 60). No difference between the men's and women's perceptions of ability was found and those who had been told the skills were acquired were more confident than those who had been told they were learned. Similar findings have emerged from studies of children as young as 7–10 years old (Eccles et al, 1993) and 10–11 years old (Granleese et al, 1988; Fazey and Keely, 1992) except that in the Fazey and Keely's (1992) study, the girls' perceived competence at gender neutral sports (swimming, tennis, rounders) was also lower than the boys'.

Of their results Lirgg et al (1996) speculate that the women in the innate condition expected to be competent at the feminine activity because, being female, they considered that they already have the necessary skills. When the activity is masculine, however, only those who are told the skill is learned believe they can do it. Men, in contrast, may believe that because a task is feminine it is easy and therefore, even if the required skills are innate, they should be able to do it. Because confidence and perceived competence have been found to predict sports participation (Eccles and Harold, 1991; Coakley and White, 1992), this suggests that if the task is considered to be masculine and if girls and women perceive themselves to be unable to master these tasks they may never attempt to do so. Whilst this cannot be concluded from Lirgg et al's study, research findings from the perceived masculine fields of maths and science suggest that it is a possibility. In maths and science, girls' confidence levels are lower than boys' in spite of school performance that indicates they are equal to or better than boys, and in Britain, the number of boys who go on to study these subjects after the age of 16 far exceeds the number of girls who do (Ernst, 1998; Walkerdine, 1998).

Negotiating femininity and physicality

Prior to age 11 and 12 the vast majority of children look forward to their PE classes with many ranking them as their favourite (Eccles et al, 1993; Fox, 1994). However, once they reach adolescence, there is a decline in both boys' and girls' participation levels that is far greater for girls (Armstrong et al, 1990; Fox, 1994; McManus and Armstrong, 1996; Armstrong and Welsman, 1997). This lesser decline in boys is likely to be because sport is a way of validating masculinity (Messner, 1992; Lorber, 1993; Chapter 1, this volume) but what of the greater decline in girls? Cockerill and Hardy (1987) suggest that this may be due to conflict between the demands of PE and the need to preserve a heterosexual feminine image. In a study of 82 teenage girls (14–15 year olds) Cockerill and Hardy (1987) asked the girls to 'Think of someone you regard as 'feminine' and someone you regard as 'unfeminine'. In what ways do they differ?' Analysis of the girls' written responses revealed three main categories which distinguished between the feminine and the unfeminine. First, the feminine girl is one who is very concerned with her outward appearance. She is slim and wears jewellery and make-up. In contrast the unfeminine girl is scruffy, wears little jewellery and make-up and wears trousers most of the time. Second, there are different personality attributes between the two. The feminine girl is sensitive, caring, weak, fragile, lady-like and proper. The unfeminine girl is rude, disorderly and loud. Third, they differ in their sport or physical activity interests. The feminine girl has little interest in sport, dislikes getting messy, prefers to be indoors and is inactive and unenergetic. The unfeminine girl is sporty, enjoys being outside and does not mind getting messy. Based on these data, Cockerill and Hardy (1987) propose that due to the demands of femininity, participating in sport is firstly not conducive to maintaining an attractive appearance (it makes you messy) and secondly, it would raise questions about sexuality as girls who are good at sports are labelled 'tomboys' and considered to be masculine and/or lesbian (see Chapters 2 and 3, this volume). As the teenage sub-culture is concerned with getting and keeping a boyfriend (the legacy of Cinderella and Snow White; Ussher (1997)), activities that lead to a perceived loss of femininity (and by default, heterosexuality) will be avoided (Cockerill and Hardy, 1987).

Whilst I see the point that Cockerill and Hardy (1987) are making, I am not convinced that teenage girls' lack of interest in sport can be explained so easily. Certainly, at adolescence, girls are consolidating their feminine identities and experiencing tremendous peer group pressure to conform to the culture of heterosexual femininity (Hargreaves, 1994) but physical appearance and avoiding a masculine/lesbian label do not comprise the whole story. Another, and I would argue more important part of the story is simply that many girls have little use for sport in the process of becoming women. Unlike boys, feminine identities are not constructed through sport, which might explain why the girls and young women in Coakley and White's (1992) study were more likely than the males to view sport as a low priority in their lives. In contrast, the boys and young men were more likely to view sport as important in the process of becoming a man. Consistent with Coakley and White's (1992) findings, Eccles (1999) has reported new results using path analysis which reveal that although both boys' and girls' perceived competence significantly predicts participation (as mentioned earlier), for girls only, the perceived value attached to being good at sport is an even greater predictor.

Thus, one reason that girls are less active than boys is because the masculine culture of sport is perceived to have little relevance to them. This has been taught to them through the gendering that occurs in our wider society and in sport, particularly the PE environment at school. It is further reinforced in the home through, as discussed earlier, more support and encouragement being given to boys to be physically active (Chapter 1, this volume). Further reinforcement comes through greater independence being encouraged in boys in general. Coakley and White's (1992) study also found that more parental constraints were in place for the girls than the boys, such as not being allowed out after dark. This had a major impact on the girls' after-school activities, including sports, because if a parent was not available to drive them, they could not go. On the other hand, the boys in the study rarely discussed such parental constraints, were allowed to be out after dark and were able to travel on public transport. In addition, a few girls who were able to take part in sports and other activities outside of school, did so on the understanding that they returned in time to help with domestic tasks. No such expectations of the boys were reported.

In addition to sport having little relevance to them, girls are also less active because in the process of consolidating a feminine identity, for most girls, boyfriends are relevant. As a result, relationships with boyfriends are often considered to be a priority and for many girls this means her interests take second place to his, as he decides what they do together as a couple (Coakley and White, 1992). As a result, the girl's sport and leisure activities are often chosen to fit in with her boyfriend's. For example, one 17 year old in Coakley and White's (1992) study used to ice skate three times a week before she met her boyfriend. Because he was not interested in this activity she stopped going:

> I started going out with my boyfriend and I just lost interest in skating really . . . We tried skating together, but he's not really keen on it . . . If it weren't for him, I think I'd go every night.
>
> (Coakley and White, 1992; p. 30)

In contrast, the young men in the study who had girlfriends did not tend to tailor their activities to suit their girlfriends and were also more likely than their girlfriends to pursue activities on their own.

Thus, decisions about sport participation or non-participation are the result of a number of negotiations that take place within the individual's life and sociocultural context and include personal goals, self-identities and self-perceptions. Ideologies of femininity are likely to be influential but it is not only, or indeed simply, in terms of presenting a suitably feminine appearance and image as suggested by Cockerill and Hardy (1987). It is through the construction of a feminine identity, which includes how physicality is perceived and experienced by girls and women, that the meaning and value of sport (and exercise) is determined for them. I would argue that sport may have little relevance or utility to the lives of girls and women because the sporty type is masculine and because of archetypal femininity in general. As a result, experiences of physicality are more likely to be concerned with attaining the ideal body beautiful than with demonstrating physical competence; hence a desire to participate in activities such as aerobics and dance (OPCS, 1992; Sports Council, 1993). Indeed, body image concerns have been found in girls as young as 8 years old (Grogan, 1999) and, as already discussed, this is a powerful motivator for women to exercise (Chapter 5, this volume). In addition, the lesser interest in sport and the greater interest in other forms of physical activity might be a reflection of what characterises, more typically, girls' play behaviour – activities that emphasise socialising as opposed to aggression and competition which characterises sporty behaviour. Eccles (1999) reports that today's girls are less interested than boys in competitive sports and more interested in physical activities such as biking and swimming as these provide ways for them to socialise and have fun with their friends. In constructing a feminine identity and in negotiating young womanhood, being sporty, therefore, is less likely to feature than recreational physical exercise does. Girls do not wish to avoid physical activity completely but their activity choices are based on what is meaningful to them and their lives. As we have seen, this decision making process is complex and can be influenced by gender and femininity in a number of ways. In order to unpack this process further let us now turn to some theories of decision making.

Predicting exercise behaviour

According to general theories of decision making, an individual's decision to take part in a behaviour will be based on a cost–benefit analysis of the advantages and disadvantages of participation. Over the last ten years or so, in the field of exercise psychology, the theory of planned behaviour (TPB; Ajzen, 1985) has become one of the most widely used theoretical models for predicting exercise participation in adults. Prior to this the research on exercise motivation was mostly descriptive (Biddle, 1995). TPB (Figure 6.1) is an expectancy-value model of choice that originally began as the theory of reasoned action (TRA; Fishbein and Ajzen, 1975) and its basic assumption is that people behave in a sensible and rational manner by taking into account available information and, in making a choice, consider the potential implications of their behaviour (Hausenblas et al, 1997). Central to the theory is intention – the implementation of a behaviour, in this case exercise, depends on the intention of the individual to do so and this has been supported in a recent meta-analysis[2] (Hausenblas et al, 1997). Intention to exercise was found to be very highly predictive of exercise behaviour as the effect size from the meta-analysis was 1.09. Intention is determined by two

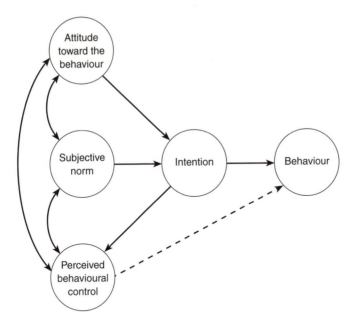

Figure 6.1 Theory of planned behaviour. (From Ajzen (1988) *Attitudes, personality and behaviour*, with permission from Open University Press.)

variables – attitudes towards behaviour (beliefs about the consequences of exercising and positive or negative appraisal of those consequences) and subjective norm (social pressures to exercise and the person's motivation to comply). In the meta-analysis the effect sizes for these variables were 1.22 and 0.56 respectively, illustrating how much stronger attitude is than subjective norm in predicting intention to exercise. According to Hausenblas et al (1997) the reason for this finding is not clear and they suggest that it may mean that, in predicting exercise behaviour, the subjective norm variable is simply less useful or that its operationalisation is limited. I would certainly concur with this because the variables in this model are restricted to the behaviour in question, in this case exercise. In fact, I consider the model to be very limited because it does not have the scope to consider the wider sociocultural factors concerning how women should look (slim and toned) or how women should behave (in a feminine appropriate manner) and how these might affect other beliefs and schema besides sport and exercise. As a result, the research approach has not been to assess how variables other than those concerning exercise influence intention to participate and influence choice of physical activity – gender appropriate or otherwise.

Later on a third variable was added, extending TRA to TPB – perceived behavioural control – the extent to which the individual believes it to be easy or difficult to proceed to an act. Perceived behavioural control is similar to Bandura's (1986) perceived self-efficacy where it is concerned with the beliefs that individuals have about the resources and opportunities available to them in order to execute the behaviour. This third variable is particularly useful for studying behaviour that may not be under the complete control of the individual (Blue, 1995). One limitation of the TRA was that it assumed the behaviour was under the individual's volitional control (Maddux and DuCharme, 1997).

Large effect sizes have also been found for the perceived behavioural control variable of TPB. Hausenblas et al (1997) found it to have an effect size of 0.97 on intention to exercise and 1.01 on the exercise behaviour itself, confirming the proposition that perceived behavioural control can influence the behaviour directly as well as by influencing intention. This also confirms the viewpoint that intention alone is not necessarily enough when the individual believes that they do not have the resources and opportunities (these can be physical as well as mental) to execute the behaviour. Differences between studies in the definition and operationalisation of the perceived behavioural control variable is problematic, however. In Blue's (1995) review she concluded that this variable had stronger predictive value for intention than for the exercise behaviour itself. One reason for this, she suggests, may be measurement issues. However, as self-efficacy beliefs influence how much effort will be put into goal achievement, persistence in the face of adversity and emotional reactions to progress (Maddux and DuCharme (1997), perceived behavioural control is surely important in assessing predictors of exercise behaviour in women given the social and psychological barriers that prevent women from exercising and the tight control of participation by the predominantly male decision makers.

Thus, overall, TRA and TPB as theoretical models have some way to go before they will be able to give us comprehensive information about the decision making process in choosing to exercise or not. How the sporty type as masculine influences women's subsequent physical activity choices cannot be determined using these models given the restrictions of the attitude and subjective norm variables to the behaviour in question and the measurement issues. Indeed, as a result of their meta-analysis, Hausenblas et al (1997) advocate further research into what they term 'moderator variables' such as gender, age and training status. However, in the case of gender, it will not be enough simply to analyse the data for gender differences because this alone does not tell us of the nature of those differences and how they might exert an influence. A more critical approach is necessary as is the use of more diverse research methods.

It could perhaps be argued that we can only attend to so many salient beliefs at one time (Ajzen and Driver, 1991) and therefore those that will be most salient will be the ones concerned specifically with the behaviour in question. But in thinking about whether or not to exercise, as with any other behaviour, we do not consider exercise beliefs and schema only. We have a whole host of decisions to make that affect sport and exercise behaviour such as health, religious beliefs, financial, and so on. As we also saw earlier, research on children and adolescents has shown that the influence of gendering is salient in task choices and, as I have argued earlier, beliefs about sex and gender are particularly salient in the context of sport and exercise. These must, therefore, be taken into account as this indicates that the process is much more complex than these two models appear to allow.

A theoretical model of activity choice

A much more comprehensive theoretical model of activity choice is Eccles et al's (1983) general model of achievement choices (Figure 6.2). Developed from the study of achievement motivation, it describes the cost–benefit analysis involved in making a decision about taking part in an activity. As depicted by the model, a whole host of factors, sociocultural as well as psychological, have a potential role to play in a person's expectations and subjective task values and self-schema, but at all stages of the model, gendering is a possibility. One of the most important features of the model is that it is based on the assumption that activity choices are influenced by the individual's interpretation of reality rather than reality itself (Eccles and Harold, 1991). Thus, choice is based on performance expectations and how important/valuable the individual *perceives* the available options to be. These expectations and perceptions of value are influenced by task specific beliefs and attitudes such as *perceived* competence, *perceived* difficulty of task and individual goals and self-schema/perceptions. These in turn are influenced by what the individual *feels* are other people's attitudes and expectations for them and by their own *interpretations* of previous achievement outcomes which are influenced by, what Eccles et al (1998) refer to as the cultural milieu and the beliefs, attitudes and behaviours of people in the individual's life (socialisers).

In illustrating how the model is applied to making a task choice, Eccles et al (1998) have posed three broad questions: can I do this task? (expectancy), do I want to do this task and why? (value), and what do I have to do to succeed in this task? (cost–benefit analysis). In deciding whether or not to take part in physical activity the answer to the question 'can I do this task?' is more likely to be no for girls than it is for boys, particularly when the activity is a sport. This is due to the culture and environment of sport as masculine (and hegemonic femininity within women's sport): girls and women have less confidence in their physical abilities unless the activity is gender appropriate or gender neutral. The answer to the question 'do I want to do this task and why?' is also more likely to be no because of the lower value placed on female participation and its lesser relevance to feminine physicality and feminine identity. Gender appropriate activities, on the other

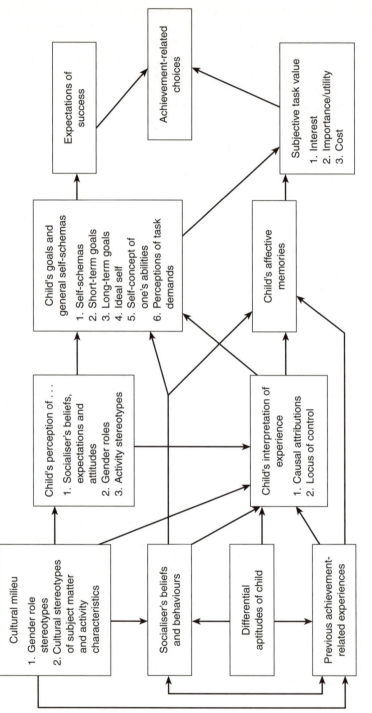

Figure 6.2 General model of achievement choices. (From Eccles et al (1998) in W. Damon and N. Eisenberg (eds.) *Handbook of child development: social, emotional and personality development, volume 3, 5th edition,* Copyright © 1998 John Wiley & Sons, Inc. Reprinted by permission of John Wiley & Sons, Inc.)

hand, such as aerobics, are relevant as this is a way of achieving the ideal body beautiful.

This argument is, perhaps, more convincing when one is evaluating sports and physical activities that can be very clearly labelled as masculine (e.g. boxing or bodybuilding) or feminine (e.g. synchronised swimming or aerobics), irrespective of whether one subscribes to these labels or not. If we imagine these to be opposite ends of a continuum, a whole range of sports and physical activities fall in between where the relevance of feminine ideologies may be more or less apparent but, as I have argued, because of the subtle pervasiveness of gendering in our society, femininity is likely to be a factor to some degree. What, then, determines how much influence this will have on the girl's or woman's choices? After all, like many other women, in spite of the questioning that began when I was a girl and continues now, I remain physically active but other women do not. Alternatively, some return to physical activity later in life, such as Judy whose school sports experience was similar to what I have described here. As a result, she did not care for sports or physical activities. However, later on in adulthood she discovered the pleasures of skiing and now revels in her physical competence on the ski run. 'I wouldn't say I'm a sporty person but I feel quite sporty when I'm skiing,' she told me. This brings me to the third question posed by Eccles et al (1998): what do I have to do to succeed on this task? and the cost–benefit analysis of the decision making process.

Central to conducting a cost–benefit analysis based on performance expectations and task value is self-schema (or self-perception). According to Eccles and Harold (1991), any given activity can be valued depending on how it represents one's view of self and the importance of the activity in confirming this view. Gendering, and the sporty type as masculine, is very important in this regard because not only does it influence the development of a self-schema as a physically active being, it also influences perceptions of the characteristics associated with particular sports and physical activities. Participating in sport will allow the individual to demonstrate skills of physical competence and if physical competence is an important aspect of the self-schema, participation will be perceived as having greater benefit than cost, thereby increasing the likelihood of choosing to take part. Physical competence can be of greater or lesser importance depending on the context within which it is being considered. For example, for Judy, mentioned above, skiing for fun and as a social activity is important to her, which has led to physical competence in that context being important too. Another example is Monica from Chapter 5 who, because of a greater awareness of the positive effects of exercise on health, joined a gym when she reached 40. For Monica, being physically competent has come to be important to her as a woman taking control of her health and her life. The benefits, therefore, outweigh the costs of overcoming her poor body image and her aversion to physical exercise.

Another example is Sandra, the bodybuilder whom I introduced in Chapter 4. Part of Sandra's self-schema is to have a strong and muscular body so participating in the sport of bodybuilding has high attainment value for her. She would like to compete in her sport but because the representations of the Physique and Figure/fitness competitions (masculinisation and sexual objectification respectively) are not congruent with her representations of self, and her identity as a woman thereby having low attainment value, she has chosen not to. For another woman who desires a slim and toned body, training with weights in the gym may have some attainment value as it would facilitate this but the representations of people who lift weights in general – largely muscular and masculine – and women bodybuilders in particular – unattractive, unfeminine and lesbian – (Chapter 3, this volume) would be incongruent with her representations of self and her identity as a woman and may, therefore, prevent her from participating in this activity.

In addition, other self-schemas will compete with a physical activity schema. For example, activities that are consistent with a woman's view of herself as a good mother are likely to take precedence over physical activities. This is due to limited time being available as it is still the case that women shoulder most of the responsibility for childcare and domestic work while they also work outside the home (Unger and Crawford, 1996). Moreover, due to archetypal femininity which contends that women put the needs of others above her own, women find it difficult to make time. Drew (1996b) found that although both women and men reported family responsibilities as reasons for not exercising, only the women reported feeling guilty if they took time out for themselves.

Eccles' model has been tested extensively on children and adolescents in the domains of sport, music, mathematics and reading (see Eccles et al (1998) for a comprehensive review). In these samples, perceptions of sport competency and the value attached to being good at sport have been found to predict sports participation as well as, if not better than, academic subjects (Eccles and Harold, 1991). It has also been found, as I pointed out earlier, that gender differences in adolescents' participation in sport is related to gender differences in their estimates of sport competency and the value they attach to being good at sport (Eccles and Harold, 1991).

The model has yet to be used to research adults and recreational exercise so much work remains to be done before we can say we have a comprehensive understanding of adults' sport and physical activity choices. It is imperative that this work is done and because Eccles' model is so comprehensive it is considered to be the most promising framework for research into sport and exercise motivations (Gill, 1994). Throughout the lifespan we continue to negotiate and renegotiate the many representations of femininity and of sport and exercise that are, and become, available to us. We are a long way from understanding these negotiations and in the meantime, girls' and women's development as physically active beings and indeed as physically and psychologically healthy beings continues to be inhibited through the sporty type as masculine and ideologies of femininity.

Notes

1 This is also true of science (McLaren and Gaskell, 1995), mathematics (Walkerdine, 1998) and computing (Grundy, 1996) subjects.
2 Meta-analysis is a particularly valuable method of assessing findings from a body of research. It differs from reviews in that whilst reviews look at the results of each study, sorting them into positive, negative and non-significant findings and then making conclusions on the basis of this sorting, this is a counting procedure. Meta-analysis, on the other hand, involves a statistical procedure that calculates the variance for the entire population of all the studies that have looked at the utility of TRA and TPB in predicting exercise participation. By treating all these studies as one single study, the effect size of intention, attitude, subjective norm and perceived behavioural control on behaviour is estimated.

7

FUTURE DIRECTIONS

In August 1999, instead of watching the WNBA league on TV in England, I was able to visit Detroit, USA, and watch the home team, Detroit Shock, play the Orlando Miracles at the Palace Stadium. This third season was to be the test of whether women's professional basketball would survive now that the novelty had worn off (Dorson, 1999). Val Ackerman, the WNBA president, considered this season 'our chance to prove that everything we've said about women's basketball being worthy is true. This is a vital year for us' (Dorson, 1999; p. 29). The increased popularity of the league shows that it is a success, that it can sell itself to the sports public. It no longer needs to be promoted by emphasising the glamour and beauty of the basketball players. I joined the boys and girls, women and men all around me who cheered the teams and screamed in excitement when their team scored. In front of me a little girl, who looked about 5 or 6 years old, waved a banner saying 'Nancy[1] is my hero'. As a result of the new images of sportswomen that this little girl is being exposed to, will she grow up believing she can be anything she wants to be? Believing she can be a professional athlete if she wants to? Will her female sporting heroes motivate her to be physically active enough to glean significant health benefits and will that continue throughout her lifespan? Will her school and other childhood experiences enable her to develop a sense of physicality that is more than a (hetero) sexualised one? One that allows her to develop a positive sense of herself as a physically active being who knows the pleasure and empowerment of bodily movement and skill, of physical challenge as well as mental, that will enrich her life?

It might be tempting to think that with so much social change in recent years, and the enormous changes in women's sport, that the odds are stacked in this little girl's favour. After all, earlier that same year when the US women's soccer team won the world cup the tremendous publicity the team subsequently received meant that soccer was very much portrayed as the sport for American girls to play. At the same time, however, as I have argued, hegemonic femininity helped to maintain the gender order. What we also learnt about the women's soccer team is that even though they play soccer, they are feminine too (Chapter 1, this volume). Then, towards the end of that same year, also in the USA, a women's professional (American) football league was launched (WPFL), but they are at the stage the WNBA were 3 years ago, using sex and glamour to promote the league. Said one of the players:

> We may not like it but we know that part of selling the league is sell-ing it as women who happen to play football. The crowd (at the promotional venue) was probably 80% men and we know we need to get them to come to the game, and if it means they come to look at us as women, that's the way it has to be.
>
> (Dohrmann, 1999; p. 25)

Thus, women who play sport still have to do so according to men's rules. However, I do not wish to end this book on a negative note. Women are pre-sent in sport in a way that they have never been. Over the years there has been and still is strong resistance to this – as I have depicted in this book. Yet, in spite of this, women's presence in sport continues to grow. Boundaries are being moved and positive change is occurring. As a result, as women run faster, jump higher, as they become more muscular, ideas that both women and men hold about female physicality will continue to change and thus challenge hegemonic femininity. After all, it was once inconceivable that a woman could play American football, just as it was once inconceivable that she could run marathons.

It is important to remember too that I began the book by reporting that more women than ever are participating in recreational sport and physical exercise. Although the numbers are still low, what becomes clear from the stories of various sportswomen and recreational exercisers presented here and elsewhere is that women are making active choices about physical activity and creating new images of active women and indeed, new images of femininity. Although these new images are often controversial, as Talbot (1990b) has written, 'Women who play sports have shown, to themselves and to others, that there is no inevitable conflict between sports partici-pation and femininity' (p. 95). In having positive role models to demonstrate this, hopefully girls' and women's participation in sport and exercise will continue to increase. As Silken Laumann, Olympic rower, has said:

> Rowing is a sport where you're really powerful, muscular and tall, and you sweat like crazy . . . There's nothing glamorous at all . . . It's great that we can be positive role models for so many young girls who watched the Olympics, and that they've found out you don't have to be small and skinny to be successful.
>
> (Ewing, 1993; p. F3; cited in Young and White, 1995; p. 46)

Alternative sport forms

As well as the increased presence of women in men's sports, women are present in other ways too. For example, alternative forms of sport have developed that emphasise a 'feminist vision of power' (Theberge, 1991b; p. 129). One example of this is women's softball which rejects the philosophy of men's sports – winning at all costs (including endangering self and opponents), elitism, social exclusion and heterosexism. Instead, developing physical skills in an inclusive, co-operative and supportive environment as well as having a good time are the principles (Birrell and Richter, 1987). In a similar vein, there are many lesbian sport organisations that adopt feminist principles and resist the masculine ideology of sport and hegemonic femininity (Lenskyj, 1994). In these organisations, enjoyment and friendship – not winning – are the main aims, in an environment that openly celebrates female physicality and sexuality. Others are concerned with the competition and winning side of sport but still reject the masculine philosophies. As one rugby player interviewed by Young (1997) explained: 'Our outlook is completely different. We can be women and really competitive, but still have the common sense not to try and kill someone out there' (p. 301).

Another example of an alternative sport form is the Gay Games. Although not necessarily feminist, its emphases are inclusion, participation and achieving one's personal best (Krane and Romont, 1997). Unlike the Olympic Games, the Gay Games are open to all who wish to participate irrespective of their ability, age, race or sexual orientation. In rejecting heterosexism, hegemonic masculinity and femininity are challenged and transformed through, for example, same sex pairs participating in figure skating and ballroom dance events. Moreover, it is not just in sport that the hegemony is being challenged. Alternatives exist in recreational exercise too, again usually through feminist organisations. For example, during the early 1990s I was privileged to be part of a London based organisation which ran a sport and exercise facility for women of all ages, colour, sexual orientation and ability. In addition, a sliding scale of membership fees and free childcare facilities endeavoured to improve accessibility to low income women and mothers respectively. Physical exercise was promoted as a way of improving health and fitness, relieving stress and having a good time in a safe, friendly and supportive environment irrespective of the appearance of the body. Young and old, thin and fat, able-bodied and disabled, strong and weak – all exercised side by side under the guidance of specially selected and trained instructors.

Similar women's and/or lesbian groups exist in Britain for hiking, rock climbing and other outdoor pursuits. In addition, projects for girls are also in existence. The Spring 1999 UK Women's Sports Foundation newsletter reports a 'life project' being run in schools in northern England for girls aged

15–16. This project is a 10 week course of physical activities and workshops run after school between 3.30 and 5 p.m. The participants choose the content of the course but typically, the physical activities include soccer, rugby, aerobics, weight training and basketball. As well as learning the physical skills necessary for these sports and physical activities the girls can also learn associated skills such as refereeing. The workshops have included topics such as team building, problem solving, self defence and communication skills.

Redefining health and physical activity

As well as improving access to sports and physical exercise through either the traditional or alternative routes, changes in the way health and physical activity are portrayed must also be part of the mission to increase physical activity levels. Indeed, changes are already underway. More recent guidelines for health related exercise, from organisations such as the American College of Sports Medicine, have moved away from the recommendation that people take part in some form of cardiovascular activity such as running three or four times a week for at least 30 minutes. This recommendation was made based on data from young men and therefore fitted their lifestyle but not that of other groups, in particular women, older people and some ethnic groups (Gill, 1999). The recommendation now is lifestyle activity – moderate activity that is part of one's lifestyle such as walking and gardening. This should be done daily for 30 minutes but this 30 minutes does not have to be continuous. It can be accumulated throughout the day in shorter bouts and still have an effect on the health and fitness of previously sedentary people. Thus, physical activity is no longer being seen solely as sport or exercise. Furthermore, in addition to lifestyle activity other leisure time physical activities are also being included such as ballroom (and other forms of recreational) dancing.

Alongside this change in the way physical activity is viewed have been changes in the way health is viewed with biopsychosocial models of health informing health research and more holistic approaches to treatment. The holistic approach includes 'responding to the person as a whole (mind, body and spirit) within the context of his [sic] environment (family, culture and ecology)' (Pietroni, 1987). Yet, although health is more than just the absence of physical and mental disease/illness, in promoting health related exercise greater emphasis tends to be given to these effects. As a result, people know they 'should' exercise for health (as narrowly defined by the health and biomedical sciences) reasons (Dean and Choi, 1996) but the statistics reveal that this is clearly not enough to motivate them to do so. More holistic and in-depth information about the spiritual and less tangible psychological correlates may be more fruitful in encouraging people to exercise more. These remain largely ignored by researchers (Berger, 1996).

Effects of, or reasons for, exercising such as 'feeling good' or 'enjoyment' are frequently reported (Berger, 1996) but we do not know what these terms mean to the individuals who report them. Do they mean feeling at one with nature whilst jogging outdoors as the sun sets? Do they mean feeling an inner peace as a result of yoga practice? Do they mean the warmth that comes from having a good laugh as a result of a shared experience with friends? These anecdotes and many other 'effects' of physical activity have been recounted to me and other researchers and need to be investigated in more depth.

Rethinking gender

Although change is occurring and boundaries are being moved, what I hope has become clear from this book is that there is no room for complacency. On the contrary. More than a decade ago, Kari Fasting (1987) outlined some future approaches for women's sport based on three approaches identified by Brekke and Haukaa (1980) for a more equitable society. To show both how far women in sport have come and how far there is yet to go let us briefly consider these. The first of these was that women become more like men and Fasting (1987) interprets this to mean, in the context of sport, that women are given the same sports opportunities as men. The increased female presence in sport, not just as athletes but also as coaches, officials and administrators, shows that this has been occurring. However, women in sport, as well as in general, still do not get paid as much as men and it is still primarily men who make the decisions so the situation remains inequitable. Under this approach, therefore, 'equality' is very much on men's terms but with the increased presence of women in positions of decision making, in time this should change.

The second approach outlined by Fasting (1987) was that women develop different models of sport that are based on female and feminine activities and perspectives. The alternative sport and exercise forms described above can be seen to be following this approach. However, these are very much still in the minority and not valued in the same way as the mainstream is. The third approach was to move away from sport as gendered. However, as is argued in this book, sport very much remains gendered.

I have argued that visible differences between masculinity and femininity remain very important for the maintenance of our patriarchal society and that this is particularly evident in sport and exercise firstly because the body is so apparent in these contexts and secondly because sport is one of the last masculine strongholds where men have been able to demonstrate their superiority over women. In our dualist culture, masculinity and femininity are viewed as opposites which are then mapped onto other opposites which then become viewed as either positive or negative, good or bad (Haste, 1993). Thus, rationality (masculine) is good

Figure 7.1 The symbol of Yin and Yang.

and intuitive (feminine) is bad. Ditto active–passive, hard–soft, and so on and so on.

In subscribing to and reinforcing this, Kane (1995) argues that in sport we are allowed to see the binary (women's sport and men's sport as different with men's sport considered to be the real thing) but not the continuum of sports people where many women outperform many men. In order to facilitate moves away from sport as gendered I suggest the following reconsideration of masculinity and femininity. In Chinese medicine, one of the two theories that form its basis is the theory of Yin and Yang. These are metaphors that describe how 'phenomena in nature function in relation to each other' (Mole, 1992; p. 22). Yang represents, for example, light, energy, expansion, male, active while Yin representations include darkness, matter, contraction, female, rest. Both have to be in harmony and balanced within the individual in order for health to ensue. The symbol of Yin and Yang is the Tai Ji symbol (Figure 7.1), which 'illustrates how Yin and Yang comprise the whole of creation, how they flow into one another and how there is always Yin within Yang, Yang within Yin' (Mole, 1992; p. 23). To me, this appears to be a much more positive and healthy way of thinking about what we in the West call masculinity and femininity. Both co-exist within an individual, both are positive,[2] one cannot be without the other and in allowing the individual to freely express both greater balance, harmony, and therefore (holistic) health can result.

For the same reasons that visible differences are so evident in sport, I believe that sport is well placed to lead the way towards a society where differences between masculinity and femininity matter less and ultimately a society of true equality. And, just as it was women who led human evolution (Choi, 1999a) I fully expect women in sport to continue to lead this change that has already begun to take place.

I am confident in my gender identity, both in and out of sports. Most people equate femininity with the softer character traits. However, I feel that assertiveness, confidence and strength of character are also integral components of femininity. Sport allows you to be proud of your gender and stand up to constant challenges faced in a gender-unequal society, while maintaining and enforcing many aspects of being a woman.

(Young and White, 1995; p. 54)

Notes

1 Nancy is Nancy Lieberman-Cline, the Detroit Shock head coach.
2 Unlike the concept of androgyny which favours masculine characteristics.

BIBLIOGRAPHY

Ajzen, I. (1985) 'From intentions to actions: a theory of planned behaviour', in J. Kuhl and J. Beckman (eds.) *Action control: from cognition to behaviour*, Heidelberg: Springer.

Ajzen, I. (1988) *Attitudes, personality and behaviour*, Milton Keynes: Open University Press.

Ajzen, I. and Driver, B. L. (1991) 'Prediction of leisure participation from behavioural, normative and control beliefs: an application of the Theory of Planned Behaviour', *Leisure Sciences* 13: 185–204.

Alexander, S. (1994) 'Newspaper coverage of athletics as a function of gender', *Women's Studies International Forum* 17(6): 655–662.

Allied Dunbar National Fitness Survey (1992) *Main findings*, UK Sports Council and Health Education Authority.

Anderssen, N. and Wold, B. (1992) 'Parental and peer influences on leisure time physical activity in young adolescents', *Research Quarterly in Exercise and Sport* 63: 341–348.

Andrews, D. L. (1998) 'Feminizing Olympic reality: preliminary dispatches from Baudrillard's Atlanta', *International Review for the Sociology of Sport* 33(1): 5–18.

Armstrong, N. and Welsman, J. (1997) *Young people and physical activity*, Oxford: University Press.

Armstrong, N., Balding, J., Gentle, P., and Kirby, B. (1990) 'Patterns of physical activity among 11–16 year old British children', *British Medical Journal* 301: 203–295.

Bandura, A. (1986) *Social foundations of thought and action*, New York: Prentice Hall.

Bartky, S. (1988) 'Foucault, femininity and the modernization of patriarchal power', in L. Diamond and L. Quinby (eds.) *Feminism and Foucault: reflections on resistance*, Boston: Northeastern University Press.

Bartky, S. L. (1990) *Femininity and domination: studies in the phenomenology of oppression*, New York: Routledge.

Bate, B. (1988) *Communication and the sexes*, Prospect Heights, IL: Waveland Press.

Bauman, B. (1961) 'Diversities in conceptions of health and physical fitness', *Journal of Health and Human Behaviour* 2: 39–46.

Bem, S. L. (1974) 'The measurement of psychological androgyny', *Journal of Consulting and Clinical Psychology* 42: 155–162.

Bennett, K. (1995) 'The role of attribution in weight anxiety and eating disorders in women', unpublished Ph.D. thesis, University of Nottingham.

Bennett, W. (1998) 'Death fear blocks female boxing plea', *Electronic Telegraph* 14 February: Issue 995. http://www.telegraph.co.uk.

Berger, B. (1996) 'Psychological benefits of an active lifestyle: what we know and what we need to know', *Quest* 48: 330–353.

Berger, J. (1972) *Ways of seeing*, London: Routledge.

Biddle, S. J. H. (1995) 'Exercise motivation across the lifespan', in S. J. H. Biddle (ed.) *European perspectives on exercise and sport psychology*, Leeds: Human Kinetics.

Biddle, S. J. H. and Goudas, M. (1996) 'Analysis of children's physical activity and its association with adult encouragement and social cognitive variables', *Journal of School Health* 66(2): 75–78.

Biddle, S. J. H. and Mutrie, N. (1991) *The psychology of physical activity*, London: Springer-Verlag.

Birrell, S. J. and Cole, C. L. (1994) 'Double fault: Renee Richards and the construction and naturalization of difference', in P. J. Creedon (ed.) *Women, media and sport: challenging gender values*, London: Sage.

Birrell, S. and Richter, D. (1987) 'Is a diamond forever?: feminist transformations of sport', *Women's Studies International Forum* 10: 395–409.

Blaxter, M. (1990) *Health and lifestyles*, London: Tavistock/Routledge.

Blinde, E. M. and Taub, D. E. (1992) 'Homophobia and women's sport: the disempowerment of athletes', *Sociological Focus* 25: 151–166.

Blue, C. L. (1995) 'The predictive capacity of the Theory of Reasoned Action and the Theory of Planned Behaviour in exercise research: an integrated literature review', *Research in Nursing and Health* 18: 105–121.

Bolin, A. (1992) 'Vandalized vanity: feminine physiques betrayed and portrayed', in F. E. Mascia-Lees and P. Sharpe (eds.) *Tattoo, torture, mutilation and adornment*, Albany, New York: SUNY Press.

Bordo, S. R. (1989) 'The body and the reproduction of femininity: a feminist appropriation of Foucault', in A. M. Jaggar and S. R. Bordo (eds.) *Gender/body/knowledge: feminist reconstructions of being and knowing*, New Brunswick, NJ: Rutgers University Press.

Bordo, S. (1990) 'Reading the slender body', in M. Jacobus, E. Fox Keller, and S. Shuttleworth (eds.) *Body/politics: women and the discourse of science*, New York: Routledge.

Bredemeier, B. J. L., Desertrain, G. S., Fisher, L. A., Getty, D., Slocum, N. E., Stephens, D. E., and Warren, J. M. (1991) 'Epistemological perspectives among women who participate in physical activity', *Journal of Applied Sport Psychology* 3: 87–107.

Brekke, L. and Haukaa, R. (1980) 'Teorin som inte finns', *Kvinnovetenskapliqt Tidsskrift* 1: 30–45.

Brustad, R. J. (1996) 'Attraction to physical activity in urban school children' *Research Quarterly for Exercise and Sport* 67(3): 316–323.

Burton-Nelson, M. (1991) *Are we winning yet? How women are changing sports and sports are changing women*, New York: Random House.

Burton-Nelson, M. (1994) *The stronger women get, the more men like football: sexism and the American culture of sports*, New York: Harcourt Brace.

Butler, J. (1990) *Gender trouble: feminism and the subversion of identity*, London: Routledge.

Caldera, Y. M., Huston, A. C., and O'Brien, M. (1989) 'Social interactions and play patterns of parents and toddlers with feminine, masculine and neutral toys', *Child Development* 60: 70–76.

Canada Fitness Survey (1983) *Fitness and lifestyle in Canada*, Ottawa: Canada Fitness Survey.

Carlie, B. (1993) 'What forces affect our efforts in development and management of the moving body', *Paper presented at the XIIth International Congress of the International Association of Physical Education and Sport for Girls and Women*, Melbourne, Australia, August 1993.

Carlson, N. R. (1995) *The physiology of human behaviour*, 5th edition. Boston: Allyn and Bacon.

Choi, P. Y. L. (1993) 'The alarming effects of anabolic steroids', *The Psychologist* 6(6): 258–260.

Choi, P. Y. L. (1999a) 'Man the hunter and man the athlete: androcentricism in theories of evolution and sport', *Psychology, Evolution and Gender* 1: 33–43.

Choi, P. Y. L. (1999b) 'Flex appeal or sex appeal?: muscularity and the female body', *Paper presented at the Millennium Critical Psychology Conference*, Sydney, 30 April–2 May, Australia.

Choi, P. Y. L. and Mutrie, N. (1997) 'The psychological benefits of physical exercise for women: improving employee quality of life', in J. Kerr, A. Griffiths, and T. Cox (eds.) *Workplace health: employee fitness and exercise*, London: Taylor and Francis.

Choi, P. Y. L., Parrott, A. C., and Cowan, D. (1989) 'Adverse behavioural effects of anabolic steroids in athletes: a brief review', *Clinical Sports Medicine* 1: 183–187.

Choi, P. Y. L., Couzens, S. and Rawdin, C. (1996) 'Media representations of women's sports: a qualitative analysis', *Journal of Sport Sciences* 14: 12.

Coakley, J. and White, A. (1992) 'Making decisions: gender and sport participation among British adolescents', *Sociology of Sport Journal* 9(1): 20–35.

Cockerill, S. A. and Hardy, C. (1987) 'The concept of femininity and its implications for physical education', *British Journal of Physical Education* 8(4): 149–151.

Cohen, G. L. (1993) *Women in sport: issues and controversies*, London: Sage Publications.

Colley, A., Nash, J., O'Donnell, L., and Restorick, L. (1987) 'Attitudes to the female sex role and sex-typing of physical activities', *International Journal of Sport Psychology* 18: 19–29.

Condry, J. C. and Condry, S. M. (1976) 'Sex differences: a study of the eye of the beholder', *Child Development* 47: 812–819.

Condry, S. M., Condry, J. C., and Pogatshnik, L. W. (1983) 'Sex differences: a study of the ear of the beholder', *Sex Roles* 9: 697–704.

Connell, R. W. (1983) *Which way is up? Essays on class, sex and culture*, Sydney, Australia: Allen and Unwin.

Connell, R. W. (1990) 'An iron man: the body and some contradictions of hegemonic masculinity', in M. A. Messner and D. F. Sabo (eds.) *Sport, men and the gender order: critical feminist perspectives*, Champaign, IL: Human Kinetics.

Cooper, K. H. (1970) *New aerobics*, Philadelphia: Lippincott.

Corbin, C. B., Landers, D. M., Feltz, D. L., and Senior, K. (1983) 'Sex differences in performance estimates: female lack of self-confidence vs. male boastfulness', *Research Quarterly for Exercise and Sport* 54: 407–410.

Csizma, K. A., Wittig, A. F., and Schurr, K. T. (1988) 'Sport stereotypes and gender', *Journal of Sport and Exercise Psychology* 10: 62–74.

Cumming, D. C. (1992) 'Discussion: Reproduction – exercise related adaptations and the health of women and men', in S. Bouchard (ed.) *Exercise, fitness and health*, Champaign, IL: Human Kinetics.

Daniels, D. (1992) 'Gender (body) verification (building)', *Play and Culture* 5: 370–377.

Davis, C. (1997) 'Body image, exercise and eating behaviours', in K. R. Fox (ed.) *The physical self: from motivation to well being*, Champaign, IL: Human Kinetics.

Davis, C., Fox, J., Brewer, H., and Ratusny, D. (1995) 'Motivations to exercise as a function of personality characteristics, age and gender', *Personality and Individual Differences* 19(2): 165–174.

De Bertodano, H. (1998) 'Taking it like a man', *Electronic Telegraph* 11 April: Issue 1051. http://www.telegraph.co.uk

Dean, P. and Choi, P. (1996) 'The meaning of exercise and health: a qualitative approach', in C. Robson, B. Cripps, and H. Steinberg (eds.) *Quality and quantity: research methods in sport and exercise psychology*, Leicester: BPS Books.

DeFrantz, A. L. (1993) 'The Olympic Games: our birthright to sports', in G. L. Cohen (ed.) *Women in sport: issues and controversies*, London: Sage Publications.

DeSouza, M. J., Acre, J. C., Nulsen, J. C., and Puhl, J. L. (1994) 'Exercise and bone health across the lifespan', in D. M. Costa and S. H. Guthrie (eds.) *Women and sport: interdisciplinary perspectives*, Champaign, IL: Human Kinetics.

DfE (1995) *Physical education in the National Curriculum*, London: HMSO.

Di Pietro, J. A. (1981) 'Rough and tumble play: a function of gender', *Developmental Psychology* 17: 50–58.

Dibben, N. (1999) 'Representations of femininity in popular music', *Popular Music* 18(3): 309–333.

Dohrmann, G. (1999) 'Running into full contact: women's football debuts', *Amy Love's Real Sports* Fall issue, 24–27.

Dorson, J. (1999) 'WNBA: Women's pro hoops comes of age', *Amy Love's Real Sports* Summer issue, 28–32.

Drew, S. (1996a) 'Subjectivity and contextuality in understanding and changing inactivity', in C. Robson, B. Cripps, and H. Steinberg (eds.) *Quality and quantity: research methods in sport and exercise psychology*, Leicester: BPS Books.

Drew, S. (1996b) 'Moving towards active living: understanding the contextual nature of barriers to physical activity', *Health Psychology Update* 23: 10–14.

Duda, J. L. (1991) 'Perspectives on gender roles and physical activity. Editorial comment', *Journal of Applied Sport Psychology* 3: 1–6.

Duff, R. W. and Hong, L. K. (1984) 'Self images of women bodybuilders', *Sociology of Sport Journal* 1: 374–380.

Duncan, M. C. (1990) 'Sports photographs and sexual difference: images of women and men in the 1984 and 1988 Olympic Games', *Sociology of Sport Journal* 7: 22–43.

Duncan, M. C. (1994) 'The politics of women's body images and practices: Foucault, the panopticon and Shape Magazine', *Journal of Sport and Social Issues* 18: 48–65.

Duncan, M. C. and Hasbrook, C. A. (1988) 'Denial of power in televised women's sports', *Sociology of Sport Journal* 5: 1–21.

Dunning, E. (1986) 'Sport as a male preserve: notes on the social sources of masculine identity and its transformation', *Theory, Culture and Society* 3(1): 79–90.

Eagly, A. (1987) *Sex differences in social behaviour: a social-role interpretation*, Hillsdale, NJ: Erlbaum.

Eccles, J. S. (1999) 'Gender differences in sport', *Paper presented at Contemporary Issues in Sport seminar*, University of Michigan, 19 November 1999.

Eccles, J. S. and Harold, R. D. (1991) 'Gender differences in sport involvement: applying the Eccles' expectancy-value model', *Journal of Applied Sport Psychology* 3: 7–35.

Eccles (Parsons), J., Adler, T. F., Futterman, R., Goff, S. B., Kaczala, C. M., Meece J. L., and Midgley, C. (1983) 'Expectations, values and academic behaviours', in J. T. Spence (ed.) *Achievement and achievement motivation*, San Francisco: W. H. Freeman.

Eccles, J., Wigfield, A., Harold, R. D., and Blumenfeld, P. (1993) 'Age and gender differences in children's self and task perceptions during elementary school', *Child Development* 64: 830–847.

Eccles, J. S., Wigfield, A., and Schiefele, U. (1998) 'Motivation to succeed', in W. Damon and N. Eisenberg (eds.) *Handbook of child development: social, emotional and personality development*, volume 3, 5th edition, New York: John Wiley & Sons.

Ehrhardt, A. and Baker, S. W. (1978) 'Fetal androgens, human central nervous system differentiation and behaviour sex differences', in R. Friedman, R. M. Richart, and R. L. Van de Wiele (eds.) *Sex differences in behaviour*, Huntington, NY: Krieger.

Ernst, P. (1998) 'Changing views of 'The Gender Problem' in mathematics', Introduction to V. Walkerdine (1998) *Counting girls out: girls and mathematics*, 2nd edition. London: Falmer Press.

Ewing, L. (1992) *Calgary Herald*, January 12, final edition, section F, p. 6.

Ewing, L. (1993) 'A level playing field?', *Calgary Herald*, 21 February, F3.

Fagot, B. I. and Leinbach, M. D. (1987) 'Socialization of sex roles within the family', in D. B. Carter (ed.) *Current conceptions of sex roles and sex typing: theory and research*, New York: Praeger.

Fallon, A. E. (1994) 'Body image and the regulation of weight', in V. J. Adesso, D. M. Reddy, and R. Fleming (eds.) *Psychological perspectives on women's health*, London: Taylor and Francis.

Fallon, A. and Rozin, P. (1985) 'Sex differences in perceptions of desirable body shape', *Journal of Abnormal Psychology* 94(1): 102–105.

Fasting, K. (1987) 'Sports and women's culture', *Women's Studies International Forum* 10(4): 361–368.

Fausto-Sterling, A. (1994) *Myths of gender: biological theories about women and men*, New York: Basic Books.

Fausto-Sterling, A. (1997) 'Beyond difference: a biologist perspective', *Journal of Social Issues* 53(2): 233–258.

Fazey, D. M. A. and Keely, P. (1992) 'Children's perceived athletic competence in sex-stereotyped physical activities', *Journal of Sports Science* 10: 623–624.

Feltz, D. L., Bandura, A., and Lirgg, C. D. (1989) 'Perceived collective efficacy in hockey', in D. Kendzierski (Chair) *Self perceptions in sport and physical activity: self efficacy and self image, Symposium conducted at the meeting of the American Psychological Association*, New Orleans, LA, August.

Festle, M. J. (1996) *Playing nice: politics and apologies in women's sports*, New York: Columbia Press.

Fishbein, M. and Ajzen, I. (1975) *Belief, attitude, intention and behaviour*, Don Mills, NY: Addison Wesley.

Fiske, J. (1989) *Understanding popular culture*, Boston: Unwin Hyman.

Flintoff, A. (1993) 'Gender, physical education and initial teacher education', in J. Evans (ed.) *Equality, education and physical education*, Brighton: Falmer Press.

Foucault, M. (1979) *Discipline and punish: the birth of the prison*, New York: Random House/Vintage.

Fox, K. (1994) 'Understanding young people and their decisions about physical activity', *British Journal of Physical Education* Spring: 15–19.

Francis, B. (1989) *Bev Francis's power bodybuilding*, New York: Sterling Publishers.

Fredrickson, B. L., Roberts, T. A., Noll, S., Quinn, D. N., and Twenge, J. M. (1998) 'That swimsuit becomes you: sex differences in self-objectification, restrained eating and math performance', *Journal of Personality and Social Psychology* 75(1): 269–285.

Gannon, L. (1998) 'The impact of medical and sexual politics on women's health', *Feminism and Psychology* 8(3): 285–302.

Gannon, L. (1999) *Women and ageing: transcending the myths*, London: Routledge.

Garner, D. M. and Garfinkel, P. E. (1980) 'Socio-cultural factors in the development of anorexia nervosa', *Psychological Medicine* 10: 647–656.

George, T. R. (1994) 'Self-confidence and baseball performance: a causal examination of self-efficacy theory', *Journal of Sport and Exercise Psychology* 16: 381–399.

Gerbner, G. (1978) 'The dynamics of cultural resistance', in G. Tuchman, A. Kaplan Daniels and B. James (eds.) *Hearth and home: images of women in the mass media*, New York: Oxford University Press.

Gill, D. L. (1994) 'Psychological perspectives on women in sport and exercise', in D. M. Costa and S. R. Guthrie (eds.) *Women and sport: interdisciplinary perspectives*, Champaign, IL: Human Kinetics.

Gill, D. (1999) 'Gender issues: making a difference in the real world of sport psychology', in G. G. Brannigan (ed.) *The sport scientists: research adventures*, New York: Longman.

Gillett, J. and White, P. (1992) 'Male bodybuilding and the reassertion of hegemonic masculinity: a critical feminist perspective', *Play and Culture* 5: 358–369.

Granleese, J., Trew, K., and Turner, I. (1988) 'Sex differences in perceived competence', *British Journal of Social Psychology* 27: 181–184.

Green, E., Hebron, S., and Woodward, D. (1987) *Leisure and gender: a study of Sheffield women's leisure experiences*, London: Sports Council/ESRC.

Greendorfer, S. (1998) 'Title IX, gender equity, backlash and ideology', *Women's Sport and Physical Activity Journal* 7(1): 69–93.

Greer, G. (1999) *The whole woman*, London: Doubleday.

Griffin, P. (1992) 'Changing the game: homophobia, sexism and lesbians in sport', *Quest* 44: 251–265.

Griffin, P. (1998) *Strong women, deep closets: lesbians and homophobia in sport*, Champaign, IL: Human Kinetics.

Grogan, S. (1999) *Body image: understanding body dissatisfaction in men, women and children*, London: Routledge.

Grundy, F. (1996) *Women and computers*, Exeter: Intellect Books.

Guthrie, S. R. and Castelnuovo, S. (1992) 'Elite women bodybuilders: models of resistance or compliance?', *Play and Culture* 5: 401–408.

Guthrie, S. R., Ferguson, C., and Grimmett, D. (1994) 'Elite women bodybuilders: ironing out nutritional misconceptions', *The Sport Psychologist* 8: 271–286.

Guttman, A. (1991) *Women's sports: a history*, New York: Columbia University Press.

Halbert, C. (1997) 'Tough enough and woman enough: stereotypes, discrimination and impression management among women professional boxers', *Journal of Sport and Social Issues* 21(1): 7–36.

Hall, M. A. (1996) *Feminism and sporting bodies: essays on theory and practice*, Champaign, IL: Human Kinetics.

Hanley, F. (1999) 'Body image in context: a critical commentary on a construct for research, theory and everyday life', *Paper presented at the Millennium World Conference in Critical Psychology*, 30 April – 2 May, Sydney, Australia.

Hargreaves, J. (1994) *Sporting females: critical issues in the history and sociology of women's sport*, London: Routledge.

Harper, V. (1997) 'Running on empty: the secret anorexia of Britain's top sportswomen', *Cosmopolitan Magazine*, November, London: IPC Magazines.

Harrison, A. and O'Neill, S. (2000) 'Children's gender-typed preferences for musical instruments: an intervention study', *Psychology of Music* 28 (in press).

Haste, H. (1993) *The sexual metaphor*, London: Harvester Wheatsheaf.

Hausenblas, H. A., Carron, A. V., and Mack, D. E. (1997) 'Application of the Theories of Reasoned Action and Planned Behaviour to exercise behaviour: a meta-analysis', *Journal of Sport and Exercise Psychology* 19: 36–51.

Helmreich, R. L. and Spence, J. T. (1977) 'Sex roles and achievement', in R. W. Christina and D. M. Landers (eds.) *Psychology of motor behaviour and sport*, Champaign, IL: Human Kinetics.

Heywood, L. (1998) *Bodymakers: a cultural anatomy of women's bodybuilding*, London: Rutgers University Press.

Hilliard, D. C. (1984) 'Media images of male and female professional athletes: an interpretive analysis of magazine articles', *Sociology of Sport Journal* 1: 251–262.

Hirshey, D. (1998) 'Soccer idols', *Women's Sport and Fitness*, July/August, 94–99, 142–145.

Holmlund, C. A. (1989) 'Visible difference and flex appeal: the body, sex, sexuality and race in the Pumping Iron films', *Cinema Journal* 28(4): 38–51.

Howat, D., Fishwick, L., and Wolfson, L. (1994) 'Sex, sport and stereotypes: children's attitudes towards the sexes in sport', *Paper presented at the British Psychological Society's London Conference*, Institute of Education, London, December 1994.

Hyde, J. S. (1981) 'How large are cognitive gender differences?', *American Psychologist* 36: 892–901.

Hyde, J. S. (1996) *Psychology of women: half the human experience*, Lexington, MA: DC Heath & Co.

IOC (1992) 'International Olympic Committee will not give in to sex tests protests', *Agence France Presse*, 28 January, Lexis/Nexis Transcript.

Jacobs, J. E. and Eccles, J. S. (1992) 'The impact of mothers' gender-role stereotypic beliefs on mothers' and children's ability perceptions', *Journal of Personality and Social Psychology* 63: 932–944.

Jones, R., Murrell, A. J., and Jackson, J. (1999) 'Pretty versus powerful in the sports pages', *Journal of Social Issues* 23(2): 183–192.

Kalb, C. (1999) 'Our quest to be perfect', *Newsweek* August 9, 52–59.

Kane, M. J. (1989) 'The post Title IX female athlete in the media: things are changing but how much?', *Journal of Physical Education, Recreation and Dance* 60(3): 58–62.

Kane, M. J. (1995) 'Resistance/transformation of the oppositional binary: exposing sport as a continuum', *Journal of Sport and Social Issues* 19: 191–218.

Kane, M. J. and Greendorfer, S. L. (1994) 'The media's role in accommodating and resisting stereotyped images of women in sport', in P. J. Creedon (ed.) *Women, media and sport: challenging gender values*, London: Sage.

Kitzinger, C. (2000) 'Women with Androgen Insensitivity Syndrome (AIS)', in J. Ussher (ed.) *Women's Health: contemporary and international perspectives*, Leicester: BPS Books.

Klein, A. M. (1993) *Little big men: bodybuilding subculture and gender construction*, Albany, NY: State University of New York Press.

Klein, M. (1988) 'Women in the discourse of sports reports', *International Review for the Sociology of Sport* 23(2): 139–151.

Kolnes, L. J. (1995) 'Heterosexuality as an organizing principle in women's sport', *International Review for the Sociology of Sport* 30(1): 61–76.

Krane, V. (1996) 'Lesbians in sport: toward acknowledgment, understanding and theory', *Journal of Sport and Exercise Psychology* 18(3): 237–246.

Krane, V. (1997a) 'Introduction to special theme issue: sexualities, culture and sport', *Women's Sport and Physical Activity Journal* 6(2): 1–6.

Krane, V. (1997b) 'Homonegativism experienced by lesbian collegiate athletes', *Women's Sport and Physical Activity Journal* 6(2): 141–193.

Krane, V. (1999) 'Challenging hegemonic femininity', in V. Krane and P. Y. L. Choi *The body beautiful and the physically active woman*, Colloquium presented at the 14th Annual Conference of the Association for the Advancement of Applied Sport Psychology, 22–26 September, Banff, Canada.

Krane, V. and Romont, L. (1997) 'Female athletes' motives and experiences during the Gay Games', *Journal of Gay, Lesbian and Bisexual Identity* 2(2): 123–138.

Krane, V., Waldron, J., Michalenok, J., Stiles-Shipley, J., and Brown, S. (1998) *Body image, exercise and eating behaviors in female exercisers and athletes*, Symposium presented at the meeting of the Association for the Advancement of Applied Sport Psychology, Hyannis, Massachusetts.

Kriska, A. M. and Rexroad, A. R. (1998) 'The role of physical activity in minority populations', *Women's Health Issues* 8(2): 98–103.

Kuhn, A. (1988) 'The body and cinema: some problems for feminism', in S. Sheridan (ed.) *Grafts: essays in feminist cultural theory*, London: Verso.

Lamb, C. S., Jackson, L., Cassiday, P., and Priest, D. (1993) 'Body figure preferences of men and women: a comparison of two generations', *Sex Roles* 28: 345–358.

Layden (1999) 'Bare naked lady', *Sports Illustrated for Women* Fall issue, 110–111.

Leigh, M. H. (1974) 'The evolution of women's participation in the Summer Olympic Games, 1900–1948', *Dissertation Abstracts International* 35, 5098A-5099A (University Microfilms Number 75-3121).

Lenskyj, H. (1986) *Out of bounds: women, sport and sexuality*, Toronto: The Women's Press.

Lenskyj, H. (1994) 'Sexuality and femininity in sport contexts: issues and alternatives', *Journal of Sport and Social Issues* 18: 356–376.

Lenskyj, H. J. (1997) 'No fear? Lesbians in sport and physical education', *Women's Sport and Physical Activity Journal* 6(2): 7–22.

Lenskyj, H. J. (1998) '"Inside sport" or "on the margins"? Australian women and the sport media', *International Review for the Sociology of Sport* 33(1): 19–32.

Lewis, M. (1972) 'Parents and children: sex role development', *The School Review* 80: 229–240.

Lirgg, C. D., George, T. R., Chase, M. A., and Ferguson, R. H. (1996) 'Impact of conception of ability and sex-type of task on male and female self-efficacy', *Journal of Sport and Exercise Psychology* 18: 426–434.

Liss, M. B. (1983) *Social and cognitive skills: sex roles and children's play*, New York: Academic Press.

Ljungqvist, A. and Simpson, J. L. (1992) 'Medical examination for health of all athletes replacing the need for gender verification in international sports. The International Amateur Athletic Federation plan', *Journal of the American Medical Association* 267: 850.

Lorber, J. (1993) 'Believing is seeing: biology as ideology', *Gender and Society* 7(4): 568–581.

Lowe, M. R. (1998) *Women of steel: female bodybuilders and the struggle for self definition*, New York: New York University Press.

Lumpkin, A. and Williams, L. D. (1991) 'An analysis of Sports Illustrated feature articles 1954–1987', *Sociology of Sport Journal* 8: 16–32.

McKay, J. and Rowe, D. (1987) 'Ideology, the media and Australian sport', *Sociology of Sport Journal* 4: 258–273.

McLaren, A. and Gaskell, J. (1995) 'Now you see it, now you don't: gender as an issue in school science', in J. Gaskell and J. Willinsky (eds.) *Gender in/forms curriculum: from enrichment to transformation*, New York: Teachers College Press.

McManus, A. and Armstrong, N. (1996) 'The physical inactivity of girls – a school issue?', *British Journal of Physical Education* 27(1): 34–35.

Maddux, J. E., and DuCharme, K. A. (1997) 'Behavioural intentions in theories of health behaviour', in D. S. Gochman (ed.) *Handbook of health behaviour research I: personal and social determinants*, New York: Plenum Press.

Maguire, J. and Mansfield, L. (1998) 'No-body's perfect: women, aerobics and the body beautiful', *Sociology of Sport Journal* 15: 109–137.

Malson, H. (1999) 'Women under erasure: anorexic bodies in postmodern context', *Journal of Community and Applied Social Psychology* 9: 137–153.

Mansfield, A. and McGinn, B. (1993) 'Pumping irony: the muscular and the feminine', in S. Scott and D. Morgan (eds.) *Body matters: essays on the sociology of the body*, London: Falmer.

Manson, J. E. and Min-Lee, I. (1996) 'Exercise for women: how much pain for optimal gain?', Editorial, *New England Journal of Medicine* 334(20): 1325–1326.

Markland, D. and Hardy, L. (1993) 'The exercise motivations inventory: preliminary development and validity of a measure of individuals' reasons for participation in regular exercise', *Personality and Individual Differences* 15(3): 289–296.

Markula, P. (1995) 'Firm but shapely, fit but sexy, strong but thin: postmodern aerobicizing female bodies', *Sociology of Sport Journal* 12: 424–453.

111

Matheson, H. and Flatten, E. K. (1996) 'Newspaper representation of women in 1984 and 1994', *Women in Sport and Physical Activity Journal* 5(2): 65–83.

Maudsley, H. (1874) 'Sex in mind and in education', *Fortnightly Review* 15: 466–483.

Mazur, A. (1986) 'US trends in feminine beauty and overadaptation', *The Journal of Sex Research* 22(3): 281–303.

Messner, M. A. (1992) *Power at play: sports and the problem of masculinity*, Boston: Beacon Press.

Meyer-Bahlburg, H. F. L. and Ehrhardt, A. (1982) 'Prenatal sex hormones and human aggression: a review', *Aggressive Behaviour* 8: 59.

Michalenok, J. A. (1999) 'Female muscle, femininity and the body ideal: negotiating cultural boundaries', unpublished Masters dissertation, School of Human Movement, Sport and Leisure Studies, Bowling Green University, Ohio 43402, USA.

Miller, L. and Penz, O. (1991) 'Talking bodies: female bodybuilders colonize a male preserve', *Quest* 43: 148–163.

Mitchell, G., Obradovich, S., Herring, F., Tromborg, C., and Burns, A. L. (1992) 'Reproducing gender in public places: adults' attention to toddlers in three public locales', *Sex Roles* 26: 323–330.

Mole, P. (1992) *Acupuncture: energy balancing for body, mind and spirit*, Shaftesbury, Dorset: Element Books.

Money, J. and Ehrhardt, A. A. (1972) *Man and woman, boy and girl*, Baltimore: Johns Hopkins University Press.

Morris, A., Cooper, T., and Cooper, P. J. (1989) 'The changing shape of female fashion models', *International Journal of Eating Disorders* 8(5): 593–596.

Morse, M. (1988) 'Artemis ageing: exercise and the female body on video', *Discourse* 10: 20–53.

Mutrie, N. and Choi, P. Y. L. (2001) 'Is "fit" a feminist issue?: dilemmas for exercise psychology', *Feminism and Psychology* 11 (in press).

Ndalianis, A. (1995) 'Muscle, excess and rupture: female bodybuilding and gender construction', *Media Information Australia* 75 (Feb): 13–23.

Nicolson, P. (1999) 'Feminist and evolutionary psychology: ideology or method?', *Psychology, Evolution and Gender* 1(1): 1–10.

Obel, C. (1996) 'Collapsing gender in competitive bodybuilding: researching contradictions and ambiguity in sport', *International Review for Sociology of Sport* 31(2): 185–203.

O'Brien, M. and Huston, A. C. (1985) 'Activity level and sex stereotyped toy choice in toddler boys and girls', *Journal of Genetic Psychology* 146: 527–534.

Office of Population Consensus and Surveys (1992) *Living in Britain: Results from the 1990 General Household Survey*, London: HMSO.

Office of Population Consensus and Surveys (1995) *Living in Britain: Results from the 1993 General Household Survey*, London: HMSO.

Office of Population Consensus and Surveys (1998) *Living in Britain: Results from the 1996 General Household Survey*, London: HMSO.

O'Neill, S. A. and Boulton, M. J. (1996) 'Boys' and girls' preferences for musical instruments: a function of gender?', *Psychology of Music* 24: 171–183.

Pate, R. R., Pratt, M., Blair, S. N., Haskell, W. L., Macera, C. A., Bouchard, C., Buchner, D., Ettinger, W., Heath, G. W., King, A. C., Kriska, A., Leon, A. S.,

Marcus, B. H., Morris, J., Paffenbarger, R. S., Patrick, K., Pollock, M. L., Rippe, J. M., Sallis, J., and Wilmore, J. H. (1995) 'Physical activity and public health', *Journal of the American Medical Association* 273: 402–407.

Pfister, G. (1998) 'Sport and gender', in A. J. Sargeant and H. Siddons (eds.) *From community health to elite sport: proceedings of the 3rd Annual Congress of the European College of Sports Science*, Liverpool: Health Care Development.

Pietroni, P. (1987) 'Holistic medicine: new lessons to be learned', *The Practitioner* 231: 1386–1390.

Pirinen, R. (1997a) 'Catching up with men?: Finnish newspaper coverage of women's entry into traditionally male sports', *International Review for the Sociology of Sport* 32(3): 239–249.

Pirinen, R. (1997b) 'The construction of women's positions in sport: a textual analysis of articles on female athletes in Finnish women's magazines', *Sociology of Sport Journal* 14: 290–301.

Pomerleau, A., Bolduc, D., Malcuit, G., and Cosette, L. (1990) 'Pink or blue: environmental gender stereotypes in the first two years of life', *Sex Roles* 22: 359–367.

Pope, H. G. Jr., Phillips, K. A., and Olivardia, R. (2000) *The Adonis complex: the secret crisis of male body obsession*, New York: The Free Press.

Powe-Allred, A. and Powe, M. (1997) *The quiet storm: a celebration of women in sport*, Indianapolis: Masters Press.

Prince, R. (1998) 'A robe is still a robe', *Sibyl Magazine* July/August: 26–27.

Prior, J. C. (1992) 'Reproduction: exercise related adaptations and the health of men and women', in S. Bouchard (ed.) *Exercise, fitness and health*, Champaign, IL: Human Kinetics.

Pugh, J. (1993) 'The social perception of female bodybuilders', in C. Brackenridge (ed.) *Body matters: leisure images and lifestyles*, UK: University of Brighton.

Richards, M., Bernal, J., and Brackbill, Y. (1976) 'Early behavioural differences: gender or circumcision?', *Developmental Psychology* 9: 89–95.

Ryan, T. (1985) 'Roots of Masculinity', in A. Metcalf and M. Humphries (eds.) *The sexuality of men*, London: Pluto Press.

Schulze, L. J. (1986) 'Getting physical: text/context/reading and the made-for-TV movie', *Cinema Journal* 25(2): 43.

Schulze, L. (1990) 'On the muscle', in J. Gaines and C. Herzog (eds.) *Fabrications: costume and the female body*, New York: Routledge.

Scraton, S. (1992) *Shaping up to womanhood: gender and girls' physical education*, Buckingham: Open University Press.

Sharkey, B. J. (1990) *Physiology of fitness*, 3rd edition, Champaign, IL: Human Kinetics.

Skuse, D. H., James, R. S., Bishop, D. V. M., Coppin, B., Dalton, P., Aamodt-Leeper, G., Bacarese-Hamilton, M., Creswell, C., McGurk, R., and Jacobs, P. A. (1997) 'Evidence from Turners syndrome of an imprinted X-linked locus affecting cognitive function', *Nature* 387 (12 June): 705–708.

Smith, J. (1999) 'Strife in the fast lane', *The Guardian* Thursday, 5 August.

Sparkes, A. C. (1997) 'Reflections on the socially constructed physical self', in K. R. Fox (ed.) *The physical self: from motivation to well being*, Champaign, IL: Human Kinetics.

Spence, J. T., Helmreich, R. L., and Stapp, J. (1975) 'Ratings of self and personality on sex role attributes and their relation to self-esteem and conceptions of masculinity and femininity', *Journal of Personality and Social Psychology* 32: 29–39.

Spencer, H. (1896) *The principles of biology*, New York: Appleton.

Sports Council (1991) *Women and sport: a consultation document*, London: Sports Council.

Sports Council (1993) *Women and sport: policy and frameworks for action*, London: Sports Council.

Stucky-Ropp, R. C. and DiLorenzo, T. M. (1993) 'Determinants of exercise in children', *Preventive Medicine* 22: 880–889.

Talbot, M. (1990a) 'Gender – a cross-curricular dimension', *Paper presented at the NATFHE Dance Section Conference*, London, 15 December.

Talbot, M. (1990b) 'Being herself through sport', *Proceedings of the Leisure Studies Association annual conference*, Leeds Polytechnic, England, 20–22 March. (Leisure Studies Association, Conference Papers No. 44).

Theberge, N. (1987) 'Sport and women's empowerment', *Women's Studies International Forum* 10(4): 387–393.

Theberge, N. (1991a) 'A content analysis of print media coverage of gender, women and physical activity', *Journal of Applied Sport Psychology* 3(1): 36–48.

Theberge, N. (1991b) 'Reflections on the body in the sociology of sport', *Quest* 43: 123–134.

Theberge, N. (1997) '"It's part of the game": physicality and the production of gender in women's hockey', *Gender and Society* 11(1): 69–87.

Thomas, C. S. (1990) 'Stress and facial appearance', *Stress Medicine* 6: 299–304.

Tiggemann, M. and Rothblum, E. (1988) 'Gender differences and social consequences of perceived overweight in the United States and Australia', *Sex Roles* 18: 75–86.

Tuchman, G. (1978) 'Introduction: The symbolic annihilation of women by the mass media', in G. Tuchman, A. Kaplan Daniels, and B. James (eds.) *Hearth and home: images of women in the mass media*, New York: Oxford University Press.

Unger, R. and Crawford, M. (1996) *Women and gender: a feminist psychology*, 2nd edition, New York: McGraw-Hill.

US Surgeon General (1996) *Physical activity and health: a report of the Surgeon General*, National Centre for Chronic Disease Prevention and Health Promotion, Division of Nutrition and Physical Activity, Atlanta, Georgia, USA.

Ussher, J. M. (1989) *The psychology of the female body*, London: Routledge.

Ussher, J. M. (1991) *Women's madness: misogyny or mental illness*, London: Routledge.

Ussher, J. M. (1997) *Fantasies of femininity: reframing the boundaries of sex*, London: Penguin Books.

Vealey, R. S. (1986) 'The conceptualization of sport-confidence and competitive orientation: preliminary investigation and instrument development', *Journal of Sport Psychology* 8: 221–246.

Veri, M. J. (1999) 'Homophobic discourse surrounding the female athlete', *Quest* 51: 355–368.

Vertinsky, P. (1997) 'Physical activity, sport and health for girls and women: issues and perspectives', *Paper presented at the Pre-Olympic Scientific Congress*, Dallas, July 1996 and reprinted in the *Bulletin of the International Association of Physical Education and Sport for Girls and Women* 7(1): 1–15.

Wackwitz, L. A. (1996) 'Sex testing in international women's athletics: a history of silence', *Women's Sport and Physical Activity Journal* 5(1): 51–68.

Walker, A. E. (1997) *The menstrual cycle*, London: Routledge.

Walkerdine, V. (1998) *Counting girls out: girls and mathematics*, 2nd edition, London: Falmer Press.

Weider, J. (1990) 'Those wonderful female bodybuilders', *Muscle and Fitness* 51(7): 6.

Welch, P. and Costa, D. M. (1994) 'A century of Olympic competition', in D. M. Costa and S. H. Guthrie (eds.) *Women and sport: interdisciplinary perspectives*, Champaign, IL: Human Kinetics.

Whiteside, K. (1997) 'A league of their own', *Sports Illustrated, Women's Sport* Fall, 31–32.

Whitson, D. (1994) 'The embodiment of gender: discipline, domination and empowerment', in S. Birrel and C. Cole (eds.) *Women, sport and culture*, Champaign, IL: Human Kinetics.

Williams, A. and Bedward, J. (1999) *Games for the girls – the impact of recent policy on the provision of physical education and sporting opportunities for female adolescents*, Winchester, UK: King Alfred's College.

Williams, L. D. and Lumpkin, A. (1990) 'An examination of the sport, gender, race and sporting role of individuals appearing on the covers of Sports Illustrated, 1954–1989', unpublished paper.

Wiseman, C. V., Gray, J. J., Mosimann, J. E., and Ahrens, A. H. (1992) 'Cultural expectations of thinness in women: an update', *International Journal of Eating Disorders* 11(1): 85–89.

Wolf, N. (1990) *The beauty myth*, London: Chatto and Windus.

Women's Boxing Page (1999 August)
http://www.geocities.com/colosseum/field/6251/jcouch.htm.

Women's Sports Foundation (1995) *Women and sport: a syllabus guide for teachers and lecturers*, London: Women's Sports Foundation.

Yesalis, C. E. (1993) *Anabolic steroids in sport and exercise*, Champaign, IL: Human Kinetics.

Young, I. (1990) *Throwing like a girl and other essays in philosophy and social theory*, Bloomington and Indianapolis: Indiana University Press.

Young, K. (1997) 'Women, sport and physicality', *International Review for the Sociology of Sport* 32(3): 297–305.

Young, K. and White, P. (1995) 'Sport, physical danger and injury: the experiences of elite women athletes', *Journal of Sport and Social Issues* 19(1): 45–61.

AUTHOR INDEX

SUBJECT INDEX

Acuff, Amy 8–9, 44
adolescents 22, 23–4, 82, 83–6, 92, 97–8; *see also* school experiences
aerobics 68, 69, 72, 75–6, 77, 86
aggression 27–8, 80
American football 96
anabolic steroids 48, 50–1, 52, 62 n3
androgen insensitivity syndrome (AIS) 20
androgenital syndrome (AGS) 27–8
athletes *see* sportswomen
Australia 31, 32

basketball 6–7, 38, 41, 80–1, 95, 96
beauty: equals health 65–7, 76; through exercise 64–72, 74–7
behaviour: gendered 5–6, 8, 86; genetic basis 27–9, 30 n3; theory of planned behaviour (TPB)86–9, 87f
belly dancing 72
Bem's Sex Role Inventory (BSRI) 26, 27
biology: female reproduction 16–17, 18, 25; physical ability 14–15, 28–30, 44; *see also* genetic disorders; sex testing
Blankerskoen, Fanny 17
body image: cultural ideal 63–4, 76; dissatisfaction 71–4, 76, 77; exercise for 64–72, 86; gender differences 9; muscularity 70–1, 74–5; *see also* bodybuilding; self-objectification 73–5; sportswomen 38–9, 44, 82; *see also* bodybuilding; weight loss 64–5, 66–7, 70, 71

bodybuilding 45–6, 62 n2; drug testing 50–1; female competition 46–51, 52, 55–9; femininity 43, 46–9, 51–4; Figure/fitness class 55, 56, 57–8, 57f, 59, 60, 61–2; masculinity 48, 60, 62 n4, 76; media coverage 50, 53–5, 59; photography 54–5; Physique class 55, 56, 56f, 58, 59, 60, 61; sexuality 53–4, 55, 58, 59, 60–1
bone density 16
Boulmerka, Hassiba 41
boxing 14, 22, 23, 24–5, 29, 43
BSRI (Bem's Sex Role Inventory) 26, 27

Canada 4, 31, 40
children 5–6, 24, 83, 86, 95; *see also* school experiences
clothing 9, 36, 39, 40–1, 48, 53–4, 81–2
competition 2, 22, 27, 80, 86, 97; *see also* bodybuilding
confidence 82–3, 89
Coogan, Gwyn 17
Cooper, Henry 25
cosmetic surgery 48, 49, 52, 64
Coubertin, Baron Pierre de 13, 16
Couch, Jane 24, 25, 26
Cullimore, Natalie 15
dance 22, 72, 80, 86, 97, 98
decision making 86–93
diving 17, 40
drug testing 50–1, 62 n3
Ederle, Gertrude 15
empowerment 38, 76–8
Everson, Cory 49

119